TEACHABLE MOMENTS

Essays on Experiential Education

Edited by

R. Dean Johnson

D1553234

University Press of America,® Inc.
Lanham · Boulder · New York · Toronto · Oxford

Copyright © 2006 by
University Press of America,® Inc.
4501 Forbes Boulevard
Suite 200
Lanham, Maryland 20706
UPA Acquisitions Department (301) 459-3366

PO Box 317
Oxford
OX2 9RU, UK

Library of Congress Control Number: 2005934183
ISBN 0-7618-3346-3 (paperback : alk. ppr.)

CONTENTS

TEACHABLE MOMENTS

Before arriving at Prescott College, I knew little of central Arizona, where the desert rises, where ocotillo and saguaro give way to juniper and pine, and where there are mountains. "Real mountains," I remember telling a former colleague. "There will actually be snow." I knew even less of Prescott College itself, its green college status and its commitment to competence-based, experiential education. I understood how drama and visual arts courses could be experiential (how could they not?). I understood how the writing workshops I would teach, which seemed experiential by definition, could be even more experiential. But how does one make a philosophy of religion class experiential? How does one make a math course, at any level, experiential? Are students really learning as much as they would in a traditional college, I wondered. Are they really retaining more?

The purpose of this book is not to argue one educational philosophy over another, nor is it to persuade the reader to change her ways. Good educators are life-long learners, however, and this collection of essays by Prescott College faculty, both former and current, is offered in that spirit. The educational philosophy at Prescott College is not the pedagogical mountaintop but, rather, one among the many peaks of philosophies with a common goal: educating students in a manner that allows them to embrace their education, to see the interconnectedness of their learning and the world in which they live, and to reach their full potential.

Like the variety of courses offered on any college campus, everything offered here is not for everyone. Consequently, the book is not intended to be read linearly. Part I features essays offering pedagogy behind various aspects of Prescott College's courses and philosophy. Part II features essays filled with anecdotes and experiences from various Prescott College courses. Neither part contains purely pedagogical nor purely experiential essays; there are experiential moments throughout the essays in Part I, pedagogy throughout the essays in Part II, and all the essays are intended to be universal in appeal.

To guide the reader in selecting which essays are most interesting or most appropriate to his field, each essay begins with a brief introduction, summarizing the work and providing some background information about its author. I encourage the reader to use these introductions simply as trail markers, to choose the most attractive essays first, and to blaze your own path through the book. You may find yourself whole-heartedly embracing some of these essays, scoffing and shutting the book at others. Either way, in the end you will find yourself, as I did after my first year teaching at Prescott College, better for the experience.

-R.D.J.

INTRODUCTION

DAVID LOVEJOY

In recounting the genesis, growth, and maturity of Prescott College's Adventure Education program, David Lovejoy's essay also recounts the history of Prescott College. Though not intended to serve as an authoritative history, the essay dramatizes several significant mileposts in the life (and near death) of a college that embraces the idea that education is a journey.

A graduate of Prescott College (BA 1973), David Lovejoy's education and experience are varied, encompassing fields such as Photography, Publications Design, Earth Sciences, and Outdoor Education. Following graduation, he continued pursuing outdoor education as a freelance professional and as an adjunct faculty member at Prescott College. He has pounded nails in New Orleans, fought fires for the Forest Service, and worked for a variety of schools and programs including Northwest and Colorado Outward Bound Schools. In 1979, he was invited back to Prescott College to serve as a full-time faculty member in the Outdoor Action/Adventure Education program, where has been ever since.

THE EVOLUTION OF ADVENTURE EDUCATION AT PRESCOTT COLLEGE: AN HISTORICAL SKETCH OF THE PROGRAM AND THE SCHOOL

"It feels good to say 'I know the Sierra' or 'I know Point Reyes.' But of course you don't—what you know better is yourself, and Point Reyes and the Sierra have helped."
-Jerry and Renny Russell (from *On the Loose*)

Prescott College has a rich and varied history that spans more than three decades, a unique story that is best traced through the evolution of its Adventure Education program (originally titled Outdoor Action). The program has changed significantly over the years reflecting the prevailing attitudes of the times, the college's financial limitations, and the interests of the students who have been involved. The undeniable common denominators that have endured the test of time have been commitments to authentic adventure, field-based activities, and experiential learning in its simplest and purest form: learning by doing.

The Adventure Education program has enjoyed and continues to enjoy a national reputation as the leader among undergraduate colleges in producing effective wilderness leaders and outdoor educators. The history of the program can be divided into three somewhat distinct eras. The first, which I will refer to as *Pre-bankruptcy years*, spanned the time between Prescott College's inception in 1964 and the bankruptcy in December of 1974. *The Lean and Mean Years* began right after foreclosure in January of 1975 and ended indistinctly about a decade later when Mike Goff, who was the prominent post-bankruptcy Outdoor Action (OA) personality, moved to the Environmental Studies program. Around that time the college regained accreditation, and the growth in Resident Degree Program (RDP) enrollment began to accelerate. The final era, which brings us up to the present, can aptly be called *Modern Times*.

What follows is a rather informal rendering of the past, based on foggy recollections, old college catalog text, and various unorganized bits of paper found in the bottoms of file cabinets and other mysterious locations.

Pre-bankruptcy Years

Prescott College (PC) was born of a symposium sponsored by the Congregational Church and funded by the Ford Foundation. The symposium's aim was to analyze higher education in America and to define alternatives that would prepare students to become active and responsible citizens of the twenty first century. Reverend Dr. Charles Franklin Parker, a participant in the symposium, became the Founding President of Prescott College. The college would help each student "develop his or her own strategy for intellectual and personal lifestyle, and promote that sense of cultural, moral, and intellectual identity that enables a person to take rational, responsible choice and action within contemporary society." Instead of supporting traditional competitive athletics, which did not foster broad participation and were limited "to a particular and often restricted dimension of activity and values," the founders of Prescott College believed that "the contemporary student needs an activity program which, while incorporating games, also gives adventure and challenge, both physical and mental, and a link with nature." The Outward Bound program model was examined and accepted as a basis for Prescott College's Outdoor Action program.

In 1965, New Zealand born, World War II flying ace, Dr. Ronald C. Nairn became president of the college as it opened its doors to the charter class at a campus on the outskirts of Prescott, Arizona (now occupied by Embry-Riddle Aeronautical University). In 1967, with twenty-five sets of backpacking equipment and six ropes, well established mountaineer and senior Outward Bound instructor, Roy Smith, was hired to direct and develop the Outdoor Action program. Mike Acebo, a young Outward Bound instructor, was granted a scholarship to attend Prescott College and assist in the program. An advisory council was formed which included such celebrities as distinguished mountaineer, philosopher and experiential educator, Dr. Willi Unsoeld. In the fall of 1968, the first wilderness-based Freshman Orientation was conducted in Sycamore Canyon and Lake Powell. This event made Prescott College the first educational institution in the nation to incorporate the Outward Bound-style program as an integral part of its undergraduate curriculum.

From a meager beginning, Outdoor Action (initially an extra curricular program) soon gained momentum, largely due to a substantial, restricted endowment contributed by the Dewitt Wallace Foundation (of Reader's Digest fame). As interest accrued from the endowment, the program, which started as little more than Freshman Orientation staffed mainly by imported Colorado and Minnesota Outward Bound instructors, quickly gained sophistication and scope. The emphasis broadened from providing adventure experiences for Prescott College students to developing intentional leadership training and integrating field programs with academic subject matter. A statement of goals and rationale that first appeared in the *1971-72 Prescott College Catalog* reflects Outdoor Action's coming of age and legitimacy:

> Man is part of nature. His evolutionary history is rooted
> in life as a hunter, nomad and adventurer. Deep facets
> of personality and emotional needs are tied to this past.
> Urban industrial society fails to meet these demands.
> Sociological theories bear on man's predicament, as do
> romantic poets and conservationist literature. While the
> benefits of the Industrial Society are immense, we have
> yet to learn to live with them, as we have yet to learn to
> live with our environment. It is our belief that through
> the medium of the mountains, the sea, the air and the
> canyons and rivers, the qualities of **style, compassion,
> integrity, responsibility and leadership** can be fostered
> and encouraged.

In the succeeding years, the program's expansion in focus was also spurred by a growing national trend toward outdoor experiential education and the growing market for qualified outdoor leaders and teachers nationwide.

In 1970, Rhodesian born Rusty Baillie, of international

mountaineering fame, was hired to instruct in, and eventually direct, the OA program. As a result, Roy Smith's position changed to Director of Challenge/Discovery, an external program for the public, operating mainly out of Roy's summer home in Crested Butte, Colorado. This program served not only as an outreach opportunity for the college, but also as an opportunity for advanced students and graduates to hone outdoor leadership skills in a professional setting.

By 1972, the Outdoor Action program was conducting activities for students in whitewater and sea kayaking, rock climbing, mountaineering, search and rescue, sailing, soaring, scuba diving, rafting, and horsemanship. Although some courses were offered for academic credit, Outdoor Action's role was still a contentious issue, often debated by the academic faculty. Most of the activities and courses in the Outdoor Action program were extra curricular. Only students in the Outdoor Education or Advanced Leadership Training (ALT) programs were able to graduate with a degree in Outdoor Action.

Qualified students and recent graduates were given major responsibilities for helping with or running field programs. By 1973, forty students served as Freshman Orientation instructors and, overall, sixty percent of the instructional staff for the Challenge/Discovery program was comprised of advanced students or recent graduates. Jim Stuckey became a member of the faculty that year as well, teaching in a new, innovative program entitled The Institute. Overall, the OA program was flourishing, operating horse stables, sail plane instruction at nearby Prescott Municipal Airport, and a full service equipment warehouse where students could check out an array of outdoor equipment from sleeping bags to kayaks.

In 1974, Rusty Baillie left Prescott College to work for the British Mountaineering Council Training Center at Glenmoore Lodge in Scotland. Northern Englishman Mike Goff, who had been involved with Prescott College as an adjunct, left his full-time job at Saint Albans Academy in Washington D.C. to take over the directorship of the Outdoor Action program.

In many respects, the Outdoor Action program was characterized by extravagance, with informal attention to risk management; however, this was consistent with operating procedures at other institutions at that time. Ironically, the college was going broke, but the Outdoor Action program was riding high in both money and activity. Largely on Dewitt Wallace's tab, Prescott College students were traveling to the four corners of the world and doing amazing things. PC students were involved in the first sea kayak crossing of the Sea of Cortez (1969), rafting expeditions through the Grand Canyon, exploration and mapping of Thunder River Cavern in Grand Canyon, and successful mountaineering expeditions to Mount McKinley and Mount Kenya. The college maintained on-call and deputized regional mountain and scuba rescue units, and Freshman Orientation groups were traveling all over the western United States, often with little or no supervision and no oversight from college staff.The

Lean and Mean Years

Things changed radically by the end of 1974. Mismanagement and the college's involvement with fraudulent investors led to a decision by the Board of Trustees to close Prescott College's doors and submit to bankruptcy proceedings. A meeting ensued in the middle of the playing field at the old campus at which over a hundred students and approximately forty full-time and adjunct faculty members vowed to continue the tradition and not let Prescott College die. The campus, including all equipment and facilities, the Dewitt Wallace endowment, the college's accreditation and even the name, Prescott College, were lost, but the spirit of Prescott College lived on.

Roy Smith, seeing the writing on the wall, had cleverly registered the name "Challenge/Discovery" under his own name. He continued to operate this program independently of the college as a business, and many Prescott College graduates continued to staff Challenge/Discovery for the years that followed.

During the spring of 1975, classes and an unbelievable number of meetings took place in faculty members' homes and, eventually, in the rented basement of the Hassayampa Inn in downtown Prescott. The new school's name became Prescott Center and later Prescott Center College. The new non-profit parent corporation became Prescott Center for Alternative Education. The Outdoor Action program continued on a shoestring budget under the leadership of Director Mike Goff and with my assistance, an adjunct faculty member at the time.

Mike Goff's unparalleled industriousness, perhaps outgrowths of years of past farm work in Scandinavia, provided the necessary survival ingredient. Somehow, courses were conducted with a minimal amount of equipment, some of which mysteriously fell into the new school's hands from the old Prescott College inventory. For several years following the bankruptcy, the school depended on minimal everything—using private vehicles for transportation on all field courses, begging, borrowing, and requiring students to provide their own outdoor equipment.

In the beginning, activities were trimmed down to only backpacking, rock climbing, search and rescue and, to a very limited extent, whitewater sports. The initial equipment inventory was comprised of half a dozen ropes, a similar quantity of helmets and backpacks, and a few tattered climbing anchors and slings. The bankruptcy court relinquished some rescue equipment to enable the resurrected college to continue to train and oversee the Yavapai County Search and Rescue Team.

Over a hundred students continued to support the surviving institution during the spring of 1975, but many of these were seniors who were trying to finish without transferring to another school. The following fall, the enrollment dropped to a depressingly low thirty-four students. It was time to tighten belts. Jim Stuckey was elected President of "the college that refused to die." Some faculty members were ready to throw in the towel while others were excited by the future prospects. By various negotiations with Jim, the faculty was trimmed to around a dozen full-timers. Many of those who were not retained full-time left town; others secured work locally and taught a course here and there for Prescott Center College as demand warranted. For those who stayed, checks for $500 were issued as an "on call" retainer.

In 1976, the college purchased the old Mercy Hospital building at 220 Grove Avenue (where the college has been located ever since), within the city limits of Prescott. Meanwhile, Mike Goff remained the sole proprietor of the Outdoor Action program. He was the true unsung hero of this era. Without his dedication, financial sacrifice, and stubborn perseverance, the entire institution would have surely perished, for it was principally the unique nature of Outdoor Action that attracted new students during these lean years. Mike not only kept the program going, but also vital and productive during this unbelievably trying time. To put matters in perspective, all faculty salaries were the same (each less than $7,000 a year) up until the 1980s when relative prosperity began to return to the school.

On the positive side, there were a number of educational advantages to austerity and constant threats to survival. For one, the college was emotionally unified by a common purpose. We had to be a family to survive; students and faculty joined as a community of learners and friends with little hierarchical distinction. Also by necessity, students assumed even higher levels of responsibility in running all aspects of the Outdoor Action program and the college in general. The graduates from these years were an impressive group indeed, unsurpassed in ingenuity, confidence, positive "can do" attitudes, and recognition that fulfillment is not necessarily attached to financial wealth. These characteristics, consequences of environment, are evident in the ensuing careers of many of the graduates from this era, many of whom are now leading uniquely innovative and entrepreneurial lives.

Mike Goff was responsible for instituting many important changes in the Outdoor Action program during this era. All OA courses at Prescott Center College became academic credit bearing, which had not been the case previously. The curriculum was stabilized, with specific courses being offered at regular intervals. The Southwest, rather than the whole world, became our classroom. With a few exceptions, all courses took place locally. Freshman Orientation was renamed Wilderness Orientation, and it took place in canyons of Arizona's rim country in the fall and either Baja California, or in various central Arizona mountains and canyons during January. The focus of Wilderness Orientation gained breadth and included not only introductions to wilderness travel and to Prescott Center College but also to the natural and cultural environments of central Arizona.

In subtle ways during this era, the program reflected Mike's own background and values. His personal journey epitomized experiential education, with a bulk of his vast knowledge and skills gained through work, apprenticeships, exploration, and experimentation. As a transplant from the English Lake District, the cultural values of humility, communalism, appreciation of craft, insatiable curiosity, reverence for natural and human history, and an acceptance of hardships and hard work were all subtly emphasized. Humor was also a big part of Mike's interactions with everyone. The effectiveness of humor in overcoming tension and in making life fun, even under dire circumstances, was a lesson that Mike continually role-modeled. In formal terms, he articulated the program's mission, which emphasized leadership development as well as a number of other virtues:

> The purpose of the Outdoor Action Program is to
> develop the capacity for leadership, to build character,
> to heighten sensitivity to the beauty of nature, to
> challenge one's endurance with rigorous exercise and
> to encourage teamwork and build trust in one's fellow
> students through the wilderness experience. The
> major objective of this program is to help students
> acquire outdoor skills at a standard of competence,
> which will enable them to pursue activities
> independently and to develop them for their own

practical purposes. These trained men and women
will play their part in the developing Outdoor
Education Programs across the nation.

At this stage, the Outdoor Action program became fully integrated
into the college's academic affairs and was given equal status with the
other academic programs. This meant that an OA representative served
on Academic Council and the program had equal voice and power
influencing future directions of the college.

Mike Goff and the students, with some help from occasional adjunct
faculty and volunteers, ran the program from 1975 to 1979. Advanced
students, graduates, and many others helped keep the program alive.
During this period, the school's enrollment grew to one hundred students
and stabilized at that level for another four years.

In 1977, whitewater rafting got a shot in the arm when the college
purchased three used Avon Red Shank rafts from the failing Southwest
Outward Bound School and an old Prescott College Yampa raft from a
bankruptcy yard sale.

In 1979, I was invited to return as a full-time faculty member in the
program, doubling the size of the full-time staff.

Jim Stuckey continued serving as president until 1983; it was a sign
of the times that, as president, he developed and coordinated the
Summer Rafting program in the Lower Granite Gorge of the Grand
Canyon as an outreach and fund raising activity. Advanced students
served in the capacity of guides for perspective contributors to the
college. The Summer Rafting program ran successfully until 1984 when
concern arose that running quasi-commercial rafting in Grand Canyon
might jeopardize educational access by the college.

The years between 1978 and 1984 were characterized by steady
development under strict financial constraints. Expansion and
diversification in the program came about mainly by hiring our best
graduates to return and teach for us on a course-by-course basis. Other
innovative courses resulted from collaborations between OA instructors
and instructors in other programs, both within and outside of the
college. Beginning in 1978, backcountry skiing, ski mountaineering,
and snow avalanche studies were added to the curriculum—partly
through the guidance of avalanche specialists from Silverton, Colorado,
where many of our winter courses took place. Alumnus Doug Hulmes
was added to the faculty in the field of Environmental Education in
January of 1979. Doug became a vital link between Environmental
Studies and Outdoor Action and helped develop several integrated

courses such as Environmental Perspectives & Whitewater Rafting and Wilderness Exploration & Landscape Studies, both of which are still in the curriculum.

Gradually, the college's financial stability improved along with equipment and vehicles. The Flieschman Margarine Corporation donated Bus Number One, a classic short wheelbase 15-passenger Thomas school bus. Board Member D.A. Bradburn donated "Brad's Buggy," our first real 12-passenger van with a roof rack. Soon we acquired new ropes, new helmets and first aid kits; we were on a roll. We even managed to buy the school's name, Prescott College, back from Embry-Riddle for one dollar.

In 1983, Ralph G. Bohrson became president of the college and Jim Stuckey returned to the faculty. In 1984, Prescott College was granted accreditation by the North Central Association of Colleges and Schools. This made a big difference in the perception of PC by the outside world. Also, new financial aid opportunities became available to perspective students and the stable, but meager, 100-student enrollment was finally exceeded. The college seemed on the brink of success.

Unfortunately, this period also holds the darkest hour in the Outdoor Action program's history. In January of 1986, four advanced students, on a group independent study, were attempting to ascend the three highest volcanoes in Mexico. The students were responsible for all logistical planning as well as contingencies and decision-making on the expedition. Student-directed studies of this nature were fairly routine during this stage of the college's development, so the fact that the field portion of this expedition lacked a faculty supervisor was not unusual.

Near the summit crater of El Pico de Orizaba (18,410 ft.), the team of three was traveling roped together (one student had dropped out due to acute mountain sickness). One of the climbers slipped and carried the others away in a long, sliding fall. Despite their attempts, the climbers were not able to successfully arrest the slide using their ice axes. The result was a high-speed descent of over 3000 feet, abruptly ending in a fall over a small cliff on to a boulder field.

The rescue was complex and extended due to bad weather and a poorly equipped rescue team. Student, Jerry Webster succumbed to head injuries (to this date the only fatality in the history of the program). Students, Gary Guller and Dave Chianchulli both suffered lost limbs due to severe frostbite and traumatic injuries.

At least three other expeditions just like this one had taken place during the preceding years, as well as countless supervised expeditions dating back to the pre-bankruptcy years. Although we had always recognized the possibilities of such a tragedy, we were not emotionally prepared, nor did we really know how to respond or how the event should affect our future. This event shook the collective soul of those in the Outdoor Action program and the college as a whole. The questions quickly turned from what had gone wrong to whether or not our style of education was worth the risk.

The good that came out of this turmoil was the outpouring of support from our extended family of alumni and friends, the rest of the institution, and the parents of the involved students. This reaffirmation was critical to our belief in the ultimate value of program goals and our will to continue.

The college, however, did not move on without change. Our liability insurance carrier dropped us soon after the accident and for more than a year we were unable to acquire another carrier. As a result, the OA program curtailed activities that were perceived as the most potentially hazardous. A temporary moratorium was imposed on rock climbing and whitewater kayaking. The program abolished all independent studies (group or individual) involving technical skills or potentially hazardous terrain, except when taking place under strict supervision of another credible and insured organization. We changed, refined, and formalized the procedures used to approve all independent studies involving outdoor activities and study in foreign countries. These independent study approval procedures, in a slightly refined version, are still in place today.

Modern Times

In 1987, Mike Goff requested a move from the Outdoor Action program to the Environmental Studies program. He proposed to continue teaching field courses, but with a new focus reflecting his developing passion for Geographical Studies. The faculty honored his request, promoting me to the position of Outdoor Action Program Coordinator. The vacancy created by these transitions also brought Rusty Baillie back to the college.

Mike's departure from the program marked the end of an era and a transition in leadership and decision-making styles. Concurrently, Prescott College began a period of first gradual and then rapid enrollment growth, with a disproportionately high level of interest in the OA program. To serve the large number of incoming students, more faculty, instructors, administrative and logistical support were required. The response to student demand is illustrated by an escalation from two to seven full-time faculty members during the five-years from 1988 to 1992. Rapid growth also forced other substantive changes. For one, the program became formal and more structured, and in the eyes of the outside world, legitimate.

In 1988, Steve Munsell was added to the Outdoor Action faculty and alumnus Robin Kelly became Wilderness Orientation Coordinator. Robin was granted full faculty status the next year, and she became instrumental in promoting sea kayaking courses by acquiring modern equipment and developing courses that integrated studies of marine landscapes and sea mammals with kayaking in the Sea of Cortez. Soon, vastly improved outdoor equipment of all types, additions in instructional and logistical staff, upgraded vans and transportation coordination, and overall improvements in field course support (including liability insurance) illustrated the college's newly found prosperity and its commitment to outdoor education. It seemed evident that Prescott College had finally resurrected itself from its own ashes and become a legitimate institution of higher education once again.

For the whole of 1988, accelerated growth consumed the Outdoor Action program and college like an incoming tide. This occurred on the coattails of a new president, Dr. Doug North, and the strong support given to the program by Resident Degree Program Dean, Steve Democker, who was a Prescott College graduate with strong historical ties to adventure education. A threshold had been broken. Prosperity replaced stagnation, creating a sense of optimism and possibility. It was also the first time since bankruptcy that self-examination and goal setting seemed prudent and worthwhile. At the same time, there was a sense of urgency.

By 1989, the program had settled on the goal of striving to become the very best undergraduate source of well-trained adventure educators and wilderness guides. Although vaguely defined, the occupational training bent was blatant. The program grew, not only in size and scope, but also through a great deal of self-analysis resulting in many changes in curriculum and advising. Basically, we were striving for efficiency in order to meet demand while attempting to balance quality with accessibility. It became apparent that the old advising guidelines were becoming ineffective. Students were fighting their way into courses without regard for sensible progressions. They were impatient; they wanted it all right now.

The task of scrutinizing our curriculum and developing new advising guidelines was initiated in 1990. After seemingly endless debate, we reluctantly decided to adopt more structured and prescriptive curricular guidelines. A clear and coherent progression was adopted and imposed on students, even though this resulted in an inevitable loss in student creativity and responsibility. This change had philosophical implications and ramifications that have lingered even to this day. It felt as if we were inadvertently usurping the foundation goals of Prescott College by telling students how to structure their education rather than giving them the freedom and responsibility to figure it out themselves.

In 1991, Steve Munsell replaced me as Outdoor Action Program Coordinator. During his four-year tenure a number of significant changes occurred that enhanced the administration of the program. As a result of growth, more administrative support and oversight was required to run an aspiring highly professional program. To this end, the Program Coordinator's responsibilities changed by reducing teaching responsibilities to allow more dedication to a multitude of administrative tasks such as risk management, budgeting, advising and registration procedures, insurance, and access to public lands.

Four years later, Steve Pace transferred over from his full-time faculty position in Human Development program to replace Steve Munsell as Program Coordinator. He brought with him twelve years of experience working for Voyager Outward Bound School as an instructor, staff trainer, and program director. During his tenure, which lasted seven years, he initiated and facilitated a number of significant changes. These changes had the effect of bringing our program into closer compliance with standards held by other professional programs. In 1996, Steve Pace gathered support for a long debated program name change to the Adventure Education (AE) program. Outdoor Action became a mile marker, to some a nostalgic reminder of "good old days," to others a dated and unrepresentative name, sounding more like a physical fitness scheme than an educational program.

Another change initiated was the addition of human relations and teaching skills training to Adventure Education curriculum. Although in the past the program had done an excellent job of training students in technical skills, a more intentional effort to broaden students' capacities was appropriate. To remedy these limitations, selected courses in human development were integrated into the AE curriculum and advising guidelines, and practical application of leadership and teaching skills were given greater emphasis within a number of existing field courses.

Old advising documents were revised and fine tuned, formalizing three competence tracks—Wilderness Leadership, Adventure Education, and Outdoor Experiential Education—and corresponding course requirements, recommendations, and progressions. Additionally, efforts were made to develop competence tracks blending Adventure Education with Environmental Studies and Human Development. The program also made a commitment to gender equity by supporting gender responsible leadership within field courses, and promoting an initiative which encourages co-ed leadership pairs for all field courses. Selected courses, like Rock Climbing for Women, Gender Responsible Leadership, and Women's Issues in Wilderness Leadership, were offered. It was hoped and anticipated that these efforts would encourage and support greater female participation in AE courses.

At this time, we also embarked on a three-year process of refining our Faculty Field Manual, establishing procedures for field operations, staff performance standards, and activity-specific safety guidelines. All of these measures were indicative of the maturing of the Adventure Education program and necessary steps in the process that eventually led to our accreditation by the Association of Experiential Education.

Current Challenges and Future Vision

The process of self-analysis is ongoing. The people who make up the Adventure Education program have changed and these transitions are reflected in our ongoing debates over identity and focus. Some colleagues have left the institution to pursue personal passions not available at the college. Mike Goff and Rusty Baillie have retired. Steve Pace reassumed his previous position as Coordinator of Curriculum in Human Development; however, he retains responsibilities of overseeing institution risk management, and that work keeps him involved with field related issues. Talented new faculty members have come onboard to fill the vacancies, each bringing unique values and perspectives.

Thankfully, in recent years the AE program size has stabilized as other programs at the college have grown and developed. Current student demand seems much more balanced with course offerings than in the past. Although, as a program, we no longer dominate the limelight at Prescott College, this is as it should be since the result has been overall institutional enhancement. The Adventure Education program remains secure and supported. Our legacy and our ongoing contributions to an array of fields—including outdoor recreation, outdoor and experiential education, and conservation and wild lands advocacy—are evident everywhere. Simply poling leaders in any of these fields will reveal the number of "Prescotteers" whom they have valued as employees, colleagues, or bosses. Our graduates are reputable guides, teachers, adventurers, instructors, guidebook authors, field researchers, outdoor photographers and film-makers, program administrators, land managers, recreational specialists, eco-tour business owners, adventure historians, conservation and wilderness advocates, and avalanche forecasters. The list goes on and on. Additionally, there are countless numbers of past students and friends of past students who have been directly or indirectly touched, and whose lives have been enriched through lifelong intimate engagement with the natural environment in the fellowship of friends, reflecting a style and elegance that originated here at Prescott College. The Outdoor Action/Adventure Education program has made a difference, and it has been one of virtue and value.

Reflecting on the past thirty plus years has an almost dreamlike quality for those of us who have lived it. The changes have been so dramatic that I find myself questioning my own recollections. In some respects the history has followed a wild, colorful, and sometimes precarious path, yet in other ways the progression seems so natural that it assumes an almost preordained quality. The Adventure Education program has grown dramatically in size, scope, sophistication, and maturity. Yet, we continually fear becoming ordinary as some of our curricular elements and processes begin to resemble those of institutions plagued by stagnation.

As educators, our challenge for the future is to identify and capitalize on the essence of what drives our passion for this slippery and elusive style of education, and in the context of our rapidly changing world, we must do so in ways that allow us to adapt and influence change with grace and conviction.

PART I
PEDAGOGICAL APPROACHES TO EXPERIENTIAL EDUCATION

WALT ANDERSON

In defining and applying the term informed imagination, *Walt Anderson writes of the myth of scientist as objective observer and the importance of listening to the stories of the land. More importantly, he presents concepts, experiences, and activities that require students to be active learners rather than passive recipients of knowledge.*

"*I coined the term* informed imagination *to describe the process of discovery and sharing that is at the heart of it all," he says. "I hope that this approach gives readers inspiration and ideas to try similar approaches since it can be used with any group of people—from young children to adults long out of formal schooling—eager to learn about nature.*"

Walt Anderson has been both guide and instructor on expeditions to, among other places, Alaska, Argentina, Australia, Brazil, Costa Rica, Ecuador & Galapagos, Kenya, Madagascar, Mexico, Rwanda, and Tanzania. He is the author of two books: The Sutter Buttes: A Naturalist's View *(1983), and* Inland Island: The Sutter Buttes *(2004). His reviews and articles have appeared in several journals including* American Birds, Ecology, Fremontia, *and* Journal of Wildlife Management. *His photography has appeared in* The New York Times *as well as several books and magazines. A professor of Environmental Studies, Walt Anderson has been teaching at Prescott College since 1991.*

INFORMED IMAGINATION: A NATURALIST'S WAY OF SEEING

A few years ago in the respected journal, *Conservation Biology*, there appeared an editorial entitled "The Naturalists are Dying Off." Reed Noss wondered, "Will the next generation of conservation biologists be nothing but a bunch of computer nerds with no firsthand knowledge of natural history? Does it follow that they will have no personal emotional ties to the land?" His article elicited more letters to the editor than at any other time during his tenure. Among the letters was one from me, in which I wrote: "The naturalist's approach, the integration of humans with the rest of nature in a passionate and ecologically sensitive way, is not yet dead in all parts of the country." I then described the approach of Prescott College, where experiential education and direct contact with nature are still encouraged, where the field naturalist does not take a backseat to the white-coated laboratory technician.

1

There are those who see natural history as an antiquated pursuit by eccentric generalists encumbered with a multitude of fairly unsophisticated tools: a hand lens, pair of binoculars, plant press, butterfly net, and the like. It is often seen as the poor cousin of the science of ecology, which is a quantitative, analytical approach that adheres to the scientific method, that replaces subjectivity with objectivity. Hard science, according to this viewpoint, provides the ecologist with detachment from human biases, hence credibility as a resource for those making management decisions. Though natural history may be recognized as the foundation of the science of ecology, more and more institutions of higher learning are relegating it to the footnotes of history, giving conservation biologists like Reed Noss plenty of reason for concern about the future of the field.

One of the key courses in the Environmental Studies program at Prescott College is the 12-credit class in Natural History and Ecology of the Southwest. The word arrangement of the title was chosen intentionally; Natural History comes first, though all of us who teach it realize that the two subjects are inextricably intertwined. From the start, we aim to dispel the myth that these are different fields, perhaps one for the dilettante and the other for the serious scientist. Together they provide a functional lens for looking at the world, a mindset that allows growing understanding of and appreciation for nature simultaneously. We reject the idea that "majors" will take one thing and "non-majors" will take another. Ecological literacy, in fact, is a key element of a good liberal arts education that we hope every student at Prescott College will achieve to some degree. In addition, the idea of scientist as objective and detached is itself a myth. Humans evolved as an integral element of the ecosystems in which they were embedded; we see the world in ways that reflect our evolutionary heritage. Understanding our origins, learning to listen to the stories of the land that had immediate relevance for our ancestors, is not only natural; it is essential as an expression of our humanity.

I assert that to develop basic ecological understanding, one needs to cultivate the habits of a naturalist. David Cavagnaro, in his foreword to my book, *The Sutter Buttes: A Naturalist's View*, wrote: "A naturalist, I think, is first a person of the Earth, a shaman really, one who feels as well as sees, one who simply KNOWS with greater depth and breadth than intellect alone can muster. Second, a naturalist is an interpreter, one who can translate the language of nature into the vocabulary of the common man, who can reach out to us from the heart of the natural world and lead us in."

To expand upon that, I would add that a naturalist is one who cultivates *informed imagination*, one who facilitates the process of seeing more, sensing connections, translating nature's complexity into deeper levels of awareness, understanding, and appreciation. A naturalist is motivated by joy and by love: joy in the search for understanding, love for the living world within which he or she is connected. Those kinds of personal connections deny the myth of objective detachment, but they also increase the responsibility of the naturalist to be true to nature, to interpret with the greatest possible fidelity to the way that things actually work. These connections and the responsibilities they bring are at the heart of ecological literacy.

Few will find access to nature's voice by sitting down and reading an ecology textbook. For most beginning college students, that would be a sentence to boredom, often leading to rejection of or at least disappointment with science. Environmental educators often speak of "developmentally appropriate" sequencing of education. You don't hit the little kids with all the doom and gloom of environmental degradation too early in their lives, or you will sever the natural connections they may have with nature and invite rejection, despair, or psychological numbing. So it is with ecology. Many ecology textbooks appear blatantly reductionist, and though that is part of the scientific approach that can eventually come back around to synthesis and deeper understanding, it is not something that is intuitively appealing to most young minds.

In my section of Natural History and Ecology of the Southwest, I want to get students to be actively and personally involved in their own inquiries in nature right from the start. Rather than immediately laying out the foundations of theory or history for a particular subject, a practice likely to make the student more of a passive recipient than an active learner, I ask the students to come ready to go to the field on the very first day of class. I assign each a different plant (e.g., a manzanita, oak, or pine) and ask him or her to use a notebook or sketchbook to "interpret your plant species. Names are not important here. Use your direct powers of observation and informed imagination to describe it as completely as possible. Use all of your senses, get to know your plant, and be prepared to share your findings with the rest of us in a couple hours."

Two hours with a plant? Surely this stretches the patience of a young person used to quick sound bites, computer bytes, and rapid gratification. Wouldn't it be easier to follow the teacher around and take notes on whatever pearls of wisdom that person might dispense to the waiting student? Here the teacher must consciously avoid being the recognized authority. The whole point of the exercise is to allow the student to discover her or his own points of access into conversations with nature. It is the application of one's senses, combined with drawing upon a certain amount of relevant background, that will lead to success with informed imagination.

The session must be long enough for the students to reach that point where they realize how little they've "seen" at first look. If they recognize this hurdle, then they can begin to look more deeply, to ask more meaningful questions (for, in effect, they are interrogating their plants). After awhile, I circulate, reinforcing them for what they have found but encouraging a closer look, an alternative lens to peer through. You don't want to interrupt a productive inquiry, but you also don't want the students to stall and give up or feel frustrated. I must be both attentive and creative here, offering suggestions if necessary or simply cheering on those happily engaged in discovery. In any case, being supportive is the operative word. The *student* is becoming the "expert" on that species.

Early interpretive efforts may tend to the superficial. Typical left brain descriptions (dimensions, colors, shapes, how leaves or twigs are arranged, whether or not they are smooth or fuzzy) and attempts at naming are common. Some students may sketch the leaves and struggle with trying to make the drawing look real. Some might try something quantitative, perhaps counting the number of needles in a bundle or leaflets per leaf. Others may develop comparisons between this species and another (often done with oaks, for example).

There are many other potential questions that could come from a lengthy interrogation. Will someone see the plant as a potential parent, as a mechanism for its own reproduction? Will anyone describe the acceptable range of physical conditions under which the plant grows (slope, aspect, soils, shade, etc.)? Will the students speculate on the functions of flower, stem, leaf, or bark? Will they see the plants both as individuals and as members of populations? Will they note the variability within a population? Will one see the insects and other organisms attracted to the species or the signs of their former presence (holes, borings, cocoons, frass)? Will someone see the plant even more imaginatively, from the perspective of a butterfly, bird, spider, cow, worm, or drop of water? Can anyone envision the roots, the underground connections, often even more important ecologically than what was seen above ground? Can a student imagine the plant as part of the hydrological cycle powered by the solar furnaces? Does anyone begin to see through time—seasonal changes, succession, the life span of the plant from birth to death? Will attempts to relate a certain species to other plants spawn an interest (indeed, a need) to come up with names as a way of communicating about it?

After the two hours of focused studies, we all assemble and go from plant to plant, while each student shares descriptions and approaches to understanding. Of course, no one student would ask all the kinds of questions that I suggested above, but through the sharing of what each found with the rest of us, most of that range of possibilities is introduced. Only *then* do I add select natural history observations or raise additional questions to promote continued ecological thinking. Hearing a multitude of perspectives is an enriching and empowering experience; there is an awakening, a growing excitement at the prospects of growth and discovery, a realization that one's own *active inquiry* can yield insights and rewards.

The seeds of ecological and evolutionary questions have thus been sown. I ask each student to follow up on this session by writing up a species account on his/her plant, distinguishing one's direct observations and questions from any information obtained from other sources. From this point on, each person is an "expert" on that plant, and everyone has begun to learn a great deal about the natural history of the common plants in the region, as well as how they relate to one another in the larger community of organisms.

Each subsequent field trip then calls upon the students in some way to expand ecological thinking and to develop a stronger sense of place within that bioregion. Recognizing multiple intelligences, I try throughout the term to employ a variety of approaches, usually experiential in some way—sampling and quantitative work, drawing, free-writes, qualitative descriptions and comparisons, worksheets with thought questions, problem-solving exercises, and the like. Text readings are typically connected to observation and experimentation in the field. I emphasize the explanatory power of evolutionary thinking, the need to be aware of scale, the relationships among organisms, and the influences we think abiotic factors (geology, soils, climate) have on ecosystem functioning (the students repeat my mantra: "Geology is destiny"). We learn how to walk into a landscape and describe it usefully with what I call the holy trinity of ecology: composition, structure, and function.

As an example of an early exercise used to build upon readings of how physical factors affect life in landscapes, I bring the students to one of the highest vantage points in the Prescott area. The students have a worksheet that invites each of them to read the landscape in the spirit of informed imagination. I ask them to work in small groups. As each person tries to articulate ideas to another, alternative views may arise, allowing a winnowing and focusing of the search for patterns and explanations. I make it clear that good questions are the starting point to finding good answers. The inquiry cycle (a user-friendly approach to hypothesis testing) becomes a familiar tool for observation and interpretation.

To demonstrate how this process works, below I provide the first questions that direct the students' attentions:

> From a high viewpoint, you can read patterns on the land. Often these represent elements related to weather, with modification by topography. Be sure that you can read a topographic map and can relate elevation, slope, and aspect to the vegetation patterns you see. Discuss the location of the city of Prescott and the implications of both the natural landforms to the city and recent land use changes (within the past 150 years) to other parts of the environment. . . . As you observe, think about the effects of seasonality; consider how different this landscape would be in another season. Include ideas about solar radiation, winds, clouds, inversions, day and night airflows, and the like.

This activity requires detective work, finding patterns and thinking about causes. It's easy enough to see the somewhat linear ribbons of the creeks that wind through town, to think about how those may be affected by paving and building, the introduction of exotic species, and patterns of cool air drainage. It may take a little more thinking and some coaching to figure out the distribution of pines in the Prescott Basin, the abundance of chaparral just over the hill on the west side of the Sierra Prieta, or the absence of mature cottonwoods on reservation lands along Granite Creek below the VA hospital. It soon becomes clear how human actions more than a century ago (mining, logging, and cattle grazing) have set up the forest for its current crisis in bark beetle infestation and fire fuel hazard.

The exercise continues after a walk to Granite Dells, a wonderland of dramatic granite outcrops next to Watson Lake. Students work in pairs to investigate ecological concepts as manifest in local flora and fauna: subjects such as micro-climate, heat transfer (conduction, convection, radiation), relationship between body size and metabolic rate, adaptations of warm-blooded versus cold-blooded organisms, the physical properties of water and air and their implications to life. If the day is windy and rainy or snowy, so much the better, for the lessons become painfully apparent. Each pair of ecological sleuths works for awhile, then shares findings with others. Connections among the various questions are created. Then each student goes home to type up answers to each question, drawing upon published material as it may amplify what was learned experientially in the field. I, of course, give abundant feedback to the students as to how effectively their answers were communicated. And so it goes on many assignments: observations, hypotheses, predictions, solutions, and expansions. The level of sophistication grows over time. The students move from budding naturalists to capable ecologists without even noticing the change.

While providing formal assignments, which serve to provide some clear structure and measurable ways of assessing learning, I also encourage students to be creative and exploratory in alternative ways. They are to document both process and product in a portfolio, to which I give timely feedback. Portfolios are highly personalized: one student may fill pages with detailed plant drawings, while another may review Darwin's *Origin of Species*. Most students use the portfolio to organize field notes, reading notes, assignments, and daily reflections on each learning experience.

In addition to having two full days per week in which to have classroom and field experiences, I schedule two four-day field trips, opportunities for immersion in an ecosystem and often ways to interact with land managers or scientists in areas of their expertise. Though there are structured activities, there are also open times where the students can apply their learning in personally selected ways. I remind them to keep their senses alert always, for practicing ecology is as important as practicing medicine or law. Inevitably, by the end of the course, students have learned a respect for and tools to expand upon the study of ecology. They have knowledge that they can apply to practical situations. Their activism can be both passionate *and* informed.

There are many exercises that I employ in this kind of class, and the processes discussed here are applicable to many age groups and many fields; therefore, let the preceding examples suffice as models of the practice of informed imagination.

Let me close by creating some visual imagery that suggests the power of the naturalist's ways of seeing. These words were designed to go with color slides, to build upon the immediate reaction that anyone would have to the images on the screen. Pictures on a screen, after all, are no more than dancing electrons; their meaning comes entirely out of our interpretation, our imagination, which is based upon our experience. You can make do here with scenes in your own mind.

Nature provides us with infinite examples of fit in form and function. One definition of beauty is good design. Who would deny that a seal in its element is a creature of exquisite beauty? Yet if you put that seal in the midst of a grassland or forest or desert, it would be hopelessly awkward and out of place. *Context is everything.* Anything well adapted to its particular niche, its proper environmental context, is a thing of beauty, and a naturalist can rejoice to be surrounded by such loveliness. Even a banana slug in a coastal temperate rainforest or a garter snake in its sinuous serenity in a shallow mountain pond should be an object of reverence, not revulsion. A well-adapted warthog, in terms of design and function, is as beautiful as a cheetah, which we more often choose to epitomize grace and beauty. So when a naturalist sees beauty, it means going beyond the superficial. It may mean seeing *into* the form and function of a grass blade, or the deciduous leaves of an oak, or the resinous needles of a pine. The naturalist sees questions and senses answers.

Learning from the land takes patience; what first we see before our eyes is not all there is to see. Take time and wait for the gift, the chance to truly see the light. Listening to the land requires attentiveness, respect, openness, and practice. To hear something, you really have to want to listen. You need to tune in to nature, tune out the internal chatter. See if you can hear the rustlings of ladybug elytra rubbing against one another or against a cactus spine. In how many ways are they communicating that we not only cannot sense, but which we lack the imagination to even guess?

If we listen and if we understand, we can hear in the vibrant chorus of geese the voice of the tundra where they nest, the traces of the fields and marshes they have visited. If we can see, the tracks of a shorebird in the mud become an international calling card, a link with a thousand-mile migration. If we can read, the rounded pebbles in a cliff become the signatures of the tumbling action of the surf rolling in and out for millennia in response to the moon's tidal tuggings. Informed imagination is a sensory vehicle without limits.

Messages are out there, all over in nature, but who these days is stopping to read them? What things are being dropped from our vocabularies because of these failures to witness?

Aldo Leopold once said that a naturalist lives alone in a world of wounds. To do anything about it, we must know what is normal and healthy. We need to know how things work, and equally importantly, we need to *care*. It is at this crossroads where ecologist and naturalist merge, where each of us, as plain citizen of the planet, needs to be able to read the stories of the land, the *natural histories* of place, and know how to act. Informed imagination is our guide.

Erin Lotz

In drawing the distinction between gender and sex, Erin Lotz does more than break down the roles women are socialized to assume. She offers pedagogically based solutions for overcoming such obstacles and illustrates, through the real-life stories of her own students, how adopting key curricular components can be successful.

"I want instructors of coed and women's courses to become more cognizant of the ways to better serve their female students," she says. "Even though my examples are set in the field, this essay is just as relevant to those teaching in the classroom."

Erin Lotz spent over a decade with organizations such as Outward Bound and the National Outdoor Leadership School (NOLS), working in both field-based and classroom leadership positions. Since joining the staff at Prescott College in 1998, she has taught across the curriculum in the Adventure Education program using mountaineering, backpacking, and rock climbing as vehicles to cultivate teaching and facilitation techniques in her students. Her course, Women's Topics in Wilderness Leadership, *covers basics of the psychology of women and its application to the field of outdoor education from both the student and the leader's perspective.*

The Littlest Birds Sing the Prettiest Songs: Wilderness Leadership and the Feminine

A van's stereo can be a potential source of contention when heading out on a road trip with a group of college-aged women. Deciding to exercise my authority as instructor and matriarch of this flock headed to Yosemite National Park, I quickly put in my favorite CD. At first, only a few in the van were entertained by the *Be Good Tanyas*, a women's trio of bluegrassy, folk music. By the end of our three and a half week intensive Prescott College course, all felt that this music was our anthem, our front-country energy source, and part of the glue that bonded us.

The chorus of the first song on the CD pronounces, "The littlest birds sing the prettiest songs," which is particularly fitting. We were eight female students and one female instructor. We set out to learn theories in women's psychology, their application to the field of wilderness leadership, and to challenge ourselves physically in a beautiful landscape. In one of our first class sessions, we studied women's physiology and noted how women are generally smaller than men (Hales 9). Though sometimes a hindrance when our work involves carrying heavy backpacks and cold weather, we shared the benefits of our lesser stature in field settings. Additionally, we discussed stereotypical social traits of masculine and feminine qualities as found in both women and men. We learned that connectedness, gentleness, and selflessness are typical of the more feminine. We affirmed that the beautiful feminine qualities that many women possess can be more valuable for wilderness leaders than size, strength, or speed. Thus, to us, the littlest birds *do* sing the prettiest songs.

Our first voyage in the backcountry of Yosemite National Park entailed a nine-day backpack through alpine terrain where we had the opportunity to summit many grand peaks including Mt. Lyell, the highest peak in the park. On day two we ascended what we affectionately called Peak 11,282. This peak was first climbed by three women in 1931, Julie Mortimer, Alice Carter, and Eleanor Bartlett. It struck us as ironic that this peak, first climbed by women, was left nameless while countless mountains less striking than her were the namesakes of male geographers, explorers, and politicians. Though women have been adventuring in the wilderness for centuries, they have been relatively invisible in history.

With stories from this Prescott College course, I will illustrate several important curricular components critical for women to become visible, as well as to thrive, on wilderness courses. These components include structure and choice, relationship building and individuation, building connection before challenge, and valuing feminine characteristics in leadership. Men may notice that many of these components would benefit males as well. True, as the generalizations are applicable to gender socialization more than sex. The words masculine and feminine apply to both men and women since we each are a balance of differing gender characteristics. Though the focus of this writing is on females, it is intended that all involved in outdoor education can benefit from the following information and anecdotes.

Structure and Choice

On day three, half our group summited Vogelsang Peak, linking arms and hollering at the top of our lungs, while the other half, at the base camp, laughed out of control, wrote in their journals, or rested aching bodies. A journey in camp, or through one's emotions, was as appropriate a learning opportunity as reaching the top of a mountain. Both groups were having worthy wilderness experiences.

The National Outdoor Leadership School suggests structure is a factor with which female students respond well. Therefore, my intention was to provide a solid structure for this course. While the more masculine tolerate, and may even prefer, a more improvisational approach, clear steps and objectives allow women to relax and settle into what is to come. I gave the students a clear syllabus with a travel itinerary as well as due dates for several reading and writing assignments. Before the trip began we had ample planning days for folks to ask questions and be well prepared. We gave structure to our hiking one afternoon by instituting an expectation of not hiking more than fifteen minutes in any one position in the line. Many women are physically slowed down by the idea of being the slowest; continuously hiking in the back of the line can be both physically and emotionally exhausting. It is as if the metaphoric weight on each woman's shoulders affects her pace as much as would additional pounds in her backpack. My student Dana found this to be true. Once she spent her fifteen minutes in the front she felt energized, capable, and yes, faster—all things with which she had previously struggled when taller, stronger men took up positions in the front of a group. Women who worry that they may slow the group are often hesitant to hike in front. That day our structure allowed Dana, as well as each of us, to experience leading the group without the discomfort of having to assert ourselves to do so.

Also critical, however, were choices—for both academic projects and physical activity days. When able to choose to go up peaks rather than have them as assigned destinations, women have a more personally affirming experience. Denise Mitten, former director of Woodswomen, Incorporated, explains, "In order for a person to internalize an experience as her own, she has to choose it and acknowledge that she chose it" (82). Clearly this approach would suit men as well. With fewer opportunities to feel empowered over their lives' paths than men have, women can find a rare refuge from this societal norm in wilderness. On many hiking days, students were given the option to choose their pace and therein honor their own body's abilities and speed. Often, Erin W. chose to hike near the front of the pack, sometimes arriving at our planned destination an hour before our last little bird. Being able to release energy through her hiking helped her to relax and focus while we were in camp.

Obviously, every academic course must have goals; however, our task as leaders is to maximize the number of choices for each individual to obtain those goals. For example, on the day previously mentioned when students chose their activity for the day, initially several of the students felt they were *supposed* to choose the more physical option. They subconsciously believed that they had no choice, that there were *pre-determined* good and bad alternatives. Others put pressure on themselves to make the perfect decision, lest they regret it later. It is important for the instructor to put a high value on each option given. Society historically has given greater appreciation to the more tangible achievements of the mountaineer who reaches the summit than to the one who descends to tend to her or his soul. If activities are given differing value, students will applaud themselves (and others) only to the degree of worth of the chosen activity.

Individuation and Relationship

The 3,000 ft. ascent of rocky terrain leading to the glacier at the base of Mt. Lyell was enough to bring some of our group to tears. Making it to the summit was becoming less desirable and less probable at our collective pace. The obvious choices were to have the group turn around and head back to camp or to continue up to the summit, leaving slower members behind. Rather than summitting or returning, we chose to *change* our goal to something that everyone was capable of and invested in. We'd make the glacier our destination, an alpine feature that none had experienced before. Together spirits rose. We were an intact group once again. We arrived at the glacier, laughed, took photos and enjoyed each other. Once all were content with our visit to the huge river of ice, we made a plan for our descent. I set a time when all must be below the terminal moraine. Students individually assessed their energy level, desire to summit, and their pace. Joy and Laura chose to attempt the climb before heading down. The three of us went up until steep, unrelenting ice kept us from reaching the summit, then hiked down joining the rest of the group, each of us satisfied as an individual and as part of our flock.

A common goal of outdoor education programs is personal growth or the development of self. Kurt Hahn, co-founder of Outward Bound, encouraged young boys to develop their identity and self through striving for self-reliance, craftsmanship, physical fitness and service. To Hahn, *individual* achievement was a key component to individual development. Carol Gilligan tells us that for women, however, identity development is encouraged by intimacy. Expecting young girls to become more independent, or more self reliant, may run counter to their natural tendencies. A young girl's primary model, from birth, is the mother-daughter relationship. She is soon aware that care taking is a large part of the feminine. Moreover, Gilligan tells us that relationship and responsibility are the moral pillars for the feminine while the more masculine make moral decisions based on rights and rules. Under this premise, most women will base fairness on a complex network of people's effects on each other rather than a more masculine system of justice based on a pre-determined right and wrong (10). The bottom line, how we relate to others, as well as care for others, is critical in girls' and women's development.

This emphasis on responsibility and relationship to others is clearly not to suggest girls and women are unable to do things on their own. Rather, the intrinsic motivation behind separation, or finding their independence, is to more capably care for others (Gilligan 7). The directive of Kurt Hahn's service founded in compassion is not alone sufficient to illustrate the fullness of a woman's care giving. From her empathetic standpoint, a female feels a personal purpose in the act of care-taking as much as the product of the care. Sara and Laura illustrated this feeling in their comments after climbing our most difficult peak, which became a short day for them but very long one for other students. They felt guilty for being safe in camp while others were clearly going to return in the dark. Sara and Laura wanted to use their own strength and energy to trade places, to take on the burden for their peers.

As wilderness leaders and outdoor educators, we can cultivate personal growth and identity development in both males and females while at the same time honoring the moral objectives of all genders through a balance of both individuation and relationship. To our group, individuation meant having personal choice, each woman hiking at her own speed, being responsible for her own camp (setup, cooking, cleanup), and becoming an expert on a particular topic to share with the group. Relationships were cultivated through providing a physically and emotionally safe environment where students felt comfortable expressing themselves to others and were given the time to do so.

Connection Before Challenge

We embarked on our intended fifth-class climbing curriculum two weeks into the course. After two rest, research, and re-supply days in Mammoth, California, we returned to Tuolumne to hike into Cathedral Lakes. Our campsite for the next five days placed us on high granite slabs overlooking Cathedral Lake and with Cathedral Peak maternally watching over us. In 1869, John Muir said of this place, "This I may say is the first time I have been to church in California" (qtd. in Moynier 358). We certainly felt blessed by the beauty surrounding us. Some also felt a nearly religious awe of the peak, which we would have the opportunity to climb on our final days.

Rock climbing can be an intimidating endeavor for any person, male or female; however, by sequencing group activities correctly women may find challenge and risk easier and more successfully undertaken. A familiar sociological model of group development suggests groups progress from *Forming, Storming, Norming, to Performing and onto Adjourning* (Tuckman 419). This model, however, was developed through the study of men's and co-ed groups. Linda Schiller suggests that the middle three stages be "altered" for groups of all women (3). Her work is in group therapy, but her theory is applicable to outdoor education as well. After leaving the first stage of polite interactions (forming), women advance to a stage called *establishing a relational base*. Only after experiencing their commonalities do women move onto the next stage, *mutuality and interpersonal empathy*. Progressing beyond simple connection, in this stage women form bonds which allow for empathetic understanding of similarity as well as difference. The previous stages allow for a sense of safety through which *challenge and change* can then be approached. In this fourth stage, women are able to more confidently self-disclose emotional issues or to try new physical and mental challenges such as rock climbing. Groups of women then progress to a stage of adjourning similar to that of co-ed groups (4). I can recall many climbing days where the approach to the climb was spent catching up on the relationships of my climbing partners. For my female friends, this sharing plays a prominent part in the success of the climbing day. The apparent "gossip" is in reality a crucial element to improve the level of intimacy prior to attempting the challenge of the climb. For my male friends, the climb itself would likely rate higher as a measure of that climbing day's success.

There is physiological evidence that connecting with friends can actually serve to reduce stress in women. When women are under stress, the hormone oxytocin is released. Rather than the typical fight or flight response, oxytocin encourages women to tend children and gather with other women instead. When a woman "tends and befriends," her body releases more oxytocin which further calms her and reduces stress. Oxytocin is one hormone released during the act of breastfeeding. This is an illustration of both nurture *and* nature further solidifying the connection between women's physiology and care taking. The high levels of testosterone, which men produce, reduce the effects of oxytocin. Men do not enjoy oxytocin's effects as women do; however, their higher levels of testosterone may better predispose them to using the fight or flight mechanism more effectively.

By the time we attempted Cathedral Peak, we had bonded to the extent that we knew the first concert each of us had attended, we had spent Dana's twentieth birthday eating cheesecake in lightning drill position under an electric sky, and each student had experienced another's empathetic arm around her at some point. One student, Sonya, reacted to this bonding in a particularly refreshing way. Back in Arizona, she had always followed her boyfriend up climbs. But during our month in the Sierra, something changed for her. Despite the fact that the mountains were bigger and we were more remote, Sonya wanted to take on lead-climbing. Her body was strong and calm, her mind clear, and her heart so proud of her own accomplishments. Sonya had had enough time to settle into our group and to feel that her peers were there to support her efforts. She felt safe enough in that connection to then put herself out on a limb (or, in this case, a flake of granite).

Timely Feedback

Feedback was shared casually throughout the course: teacher to student, student to teacher, student to student, and student to herself. The feedback most dreaded was the inner voice telling us that we were not doing well, we were not strong or fast. We often joked that this was an audio tape that plays over and over unless we can figure out how to hit "auto-reverse" and listen to the flip side, the positive inner-voice. At certain points in the trip we all had a hard time finding that button on our own. For women more than men, external reinforcement is often critical. Many girls and women rely on others to form a concept of self as they find it hard to trust the perspective from within. Joy, for example, was in the middle of a tough section of a climb. She called out that she wasn't going to be able to "pull the move" and needed help rigging an alternative. My reply was not that I would come bail her out, but rather that I knew she could do it and she needed to try again. In minutes she appeared over the crest of rock proud for having succeeded. Nothing in her ability had changed. Only her self-concept.

Media has contributed to this focus on external perceptions. Women are consistently, though often unconsciously, encouraged to change their actions and appearance to please others. We see pictures on TV and in magazines of how we are supposed to look. Soap operas and movies show us how we are to act. The disappointing comparison of ourselves to the unrealistic media image of women is a powerful and unavoidable source of feedback.

Our own psychology, however, contributes as well. With relationship and connection so important to our own self-identity, knowing how we are measuring up to others (male and female) is a clue to the potential for alliance. Without that alliance, our identity of self is left in the balance, an area for uncertainty. Instructors, as well as fellow expedition members, can benefit female students by simply dispelling the uncertainty. If she is doing well, tell the student. Additionally, if she has a specific area for achievable improvement, let her know that as well. If we have the tools and information to better create our connections—whether in love, friendship, or professionally—as a result our sense of self can be enhanced as well.

Valuing the Feminine End of the Feminine/Masculine Continuum

Tara is a storyteller. Sonya doles out hugs without hesitation. Sara doesn't pass gas or belch in public. Joy keeps her stuff clean and tidy. Shana enjoys when others join her in processing her thoughts. Dana always has an open ear. Laura heats water in the morning for others and offers up her down jacket to those colder than she. Erin W. allows her weakness to show and interprets it to us with ultimate strength. These are not necessarily characteristics held solely by women, but they are traits that add to each of these women's individual style as a student and a leader. As is so evident in groups, each student is made up of many socialized characteristics that fall in different places on a feminine/masculine continuum. Traditionally, however, the field of outdoor education has valued the more masculine characteristics: adventurousness, risk taking, ambition, self-confidence, independence, and self-reliance. Incorporating inherently feminine tendencies into women's (as well as men's) leadership style allows them to lead more confidently, capably, and authentically.

In a more feminine environment, to show ones' vulnerability as well as to put one's energy into caring for another is celebrated. A leader tries not to answer all questions independently or, for example, to navigate *for* the group. Rather, she shares information and tasks and navigates *with* the group. Women for years have been socialized to take supportive roles such as wife, nurse, and secretary (Wittmer 174). In this field, women have often acted as the support system for men's adventures. Hundreds of years ago, women were cooking or sewing to support mountaineering expeditions. Today, female students on adventure education courses offer a new gift. They are repeatedly the ones to open the doors to personal disclosure. Though both genders have a need for an emotional outlet, it is usually women who more publicly express their emotions. Without necessarily being verbalized, women's ability to express themselves can be a relief to male students. Women are doing much of the work to create emotionally safe environments and to provide a place for pent up frustrations, fears, or worries present in all members. It is essential that we start to recognize this as truly important work—as important as leading a climb, as carrying a heavy pack or as arriving in camp first. Cultivating a healthy emotional environment serves a need for *all* in a group. This is leadership.

Tara presented a workshop on the loss of girls' voices at adolescence. Her teaching style addressed her topic so appropriately. Rather than report information to us, she encouraged us to tell our own tales of childhood and adolescence. Each point she made led seamlessly out of the last persons' story. She leaned in and met us with sincere eye contact. She smiled at funny examples and showed empathy to the sadder stories. She was effectively leading us to an understanding of adolescent girls in a very feminine manner. She encouraged communication and emotion; two components that speak volumes to women.

Sure, there will be tasks to be done and decisions to be made in an assertive, timely fashion (first aid situations or mountaineering days for example). Men do not have the monopoly on these characteristics, however. Women should feel comfortable moving around on the continuum of masculine and feminine traits. Jill Lawrence, a talented veteran climber and outdoor educator, joined our group for our ascent of Cathedral Peak. At the base of the climb, one student's nerves made her flustered, hesitant, and teary-eyed. In her British accent, Jill eventually said something to the effect of, "Well, Love, we don't have time for that, and it's not getting you anywhere. So get ready and tie in." Jill's compassionate, yet no-nonsense demeanor was both appreciated and truly respected by the students. She helped the student overcome her "self-sabotage" and their trio climbed the 700 foot granite monolith in a timely and safe manner.

Studies show that men are more accepted when they integrate feminine styles into their leadership. Conversely, when women take on masculine characteristics, they are perceived as acting incongruently with their nature and, therefore, inappropriately (Wittmer 174). How, then,

can women be authentic leaders? Debra J. Jordan speaks of
Transformational Leadership, where power is disseminated to the group
members to accomplish tasks. Because women see leadership more as a
dynamic *role* than a static *position*, it is often easier to share
responsibilities and allow the person with strength in a particular area to
step forward when appropriate (62).

Immediately after the completion of the course, one student, Joy,
enrolled in the most technical course offered through the Adventure
Education program at Prescott College. In recent years, this course has
appealed to very few women and very few have had the skills to enter the
course. (She was one of only two females in the class.) Nevertheless, Joy
is confidently entering into a profession where she may someday find
herself at the top of mountains named after her, the mark of a capable
woman no longer invisible.

Conclusion

The final assignment for this course was to choreograph a slide show
for Prescott College allowing us to share our learning with the larger
community. Beautiful journal entries were read by the students with
awe-inspiring photographs as the backdrop. We then invited the
audience to ask us questions. Students were exceedingly eloquent,
charismatic, and expressive. We were almost immediately asked to list
actions leaders can take to empower female students. Both the students
and myself were nearly stumped by this particular question. Though we
had certainly achieved a higher level of empowerment, it was difficult to
parsimoniously articulate to others what we had done. Though the
question motivated me to begin writing this essay, I believe that a
definitive list is impossible to compile. That said, sharing our intentions
for the trip does provide insight for empowering anyone struggling to
separate gender roles from sex; therefore, our intentions included:
- Providing both structure and choice
- Cultivating both individuation and relationship
- Experiencing connection before challenge
- Giving timely feedback
- Valuing the feminine traits in leadership

Leaders should, however, not stop here. We must continue to learn
about gender psychology and its application to wilderness leadership and
outdoor education.

Women can be competent backcountry travelers and wilderness
leaders without forcing the more masculine characteristics.

Furthermore, it is when women are empowered to be their true, authentic selves that they will be more inclined to take on challenges such as high-risk activities or more technical tasks. By giving structure and choice, by cultivating relationship prior to challenge, and by supporting with positive feedback, we can help our female students succeed. We can allow our littlest birds to sing their prettiest songs.

Works Cited

Gilligan, Carol. *In a Different Voice*. Cambridge: Harvard U P: 1982.

Hales, Dianne. *Just Like A Woman*. New York: Bantam, 2000.

Jordan, Debra J. "Effective Leadership for Girls and Women in Outdoor Recreation." *Journal of Physical Education, Recreation and Dance*. Feb. 1992: 61-4.

Mitten, Denise. "A Philosophical Basis for a Women's Outdoor Adventure Program." *Women's Voices in Experiential Education*. Ed. Karen Warren. Dubuque: Kendall Hunt, 1996. 78-84.

Moynier, John. *Climbing in California: The High Sierra*. Guilford: Globe Pequot, 2002.

Schiller, Linda Y. *Social Work with Groups*. 20.3 (1997) < http://www.haworthpress.com/web/SWG/ >.

Tuckman, BW and MA Jensen. "Stages of Small Group Development Revisited." *Group and Organizational Studies*. 2.4 (1977): 419-27.

Wittmer, Carrie. "Leadership and Gender-role Congruency: A Guide for Wilderness and Outdoor Practitioners." *The Journal of Experiential Education*. 24.3 (2001): 173-78.

RANDALL AMSTER

In arguing that the manner in which a subject is taught is as important, if not more so, than the subject itself, Randall Amster provides the impetus for a pedagogy heavy in experience and participation. Through the lens of a professor of Peace Studies & Social Thought, and against the backdrop of traditional education, Amster illustrates both the repressive and emancipatory potential of teaching methods before sharing his experience when applying experiential methods inside (and outside) the classroom.

"Education should be more than just a goal," he says, "but a way of 'being in the world' that promotes right relations both among humans and with the natural environment. This includes helping to make concepts such as justice, peace, and ecology part of the everyday experience of students, extending the workings of the classroom far beyond the schoolhouse walls."

Randall Amster received his doctorate in Justice Studies from Arizona State University. He has worked as an attorney and a judicial clerk and, since 2001, taught at Prescott College. His scholarly work and essays have appeared widely in journals and newspapers including The Arizona Republic, Contemporary Justice Review, Anarchist Studies, *and* Social Justice.

A THOUSAND FLOWERS: PEDAGOGIES FOR PEACE AND SOCIAL JUSTICE

Since that fateful morning of September 11, 2001, the role of Peace Studies as an area of educational emphasis has taken on a new relevance. Previously seen as, perhaps, laudable at best and quixotic at worst, the study of peace has now found itself at the center of critical inquiries and classroom discussions across a wide spectrum of academic disciplines. Through the resurgence of events such as teach-ins, rallies, marches, and youth conferences, students and proponents of peace have been presented with myriad opportunities to explore the meanings and methods of concepts such as militarism, pacifism, structural violence, restorative justice, protest policing, and passive resistance. Yet while such opportunities have often presented important "teachable moments" and yielded positive pedagogical results, there has also been a noticeable sense that much remains to be done.

In this light, it has become clear that peace as a *concept* and peace as a *practice* are related but distinct aims. Peace scholars have accordingly distinguished between "negative peace" (the rejection of or opposition to warfare and violence) and "positive peace" (the promotion of harmonious and egalitarian alternatives) in attempting to bridge the gap from ideas to actions (Barash 220). Pacifist projects thus often center not merely on the abolition of overt violence, but on the establishment of mechanisms to affirmatively promote social justice and peaceful relations. In so doing, one of the fundamental cornerstones of such endeavors has always been *education*, both as a device for critiquing forms of authority and power that contribute to violent outcomes and as a venue for developing skills that enable the appearance of positive alternatives.

In considering the implications of this historical moment—both positive and negative—it is useful to recall that while many new challenges have manifested, it is still the case that the issues of this day often mirror those of the recent past. David Barash concludes, "Militarism, violence, and the misdirection of national resources [still] call for opposition. Denial of human rights, of economic fairness, and of ecological sustainability all demand redress. There is need for creative and empathic efforts to envision and promote a peaceful world" (226). For many, this is where the notion of pedagogy has salience as a tool for opening doors of creative empathy that might point the way toward a future of peace and justice and away from the brink of annihilation and despair. As such, proponents of critical pedagogy have generally embraced peace education and social justice as cornerstones of an improved present and a brighter future.

The aim of this essay is to explore the implications of such practices for promoting peace and social justice through both theoretical expositions and practical illustrations. Utilizing a framework of *goals*, *activities*, and *evaluation* for developing the argument, I contend that educational methods are equally if not more important than the substance of what is taught in academic settings.

Goals: De-schooling, Emancipating, and Letting a Thousand Flowers Bloom

Proponents of critical pedagogy, such as Larry J. Fisk and Maurrianne Adams, have generally embraced peace education and social justice as cornerstones of promoting positive change. In many respects it is easy to see why this is so, given the centrality of education in every individual's development and in every culture's ability to survive. Of course, education in its broadest sense can be a double-edged sword, comprising not only *liberatory* impulses but *authoritarian* ones as well. Sadly, many of us know all too well the normative strictures of the educational system, the compulsory nature of public school, and the sense of the teacher as a "secular priest" (Illich 46). In this sense, there are strong reasons to infer that education as a broad concept carries with it both repressive and emancipatory potentials.

As Ivan Illich explains in his classic work, *Deschooling Society*, the dark side of education at times becomes even more apparent as one moves further up the scholastic ladder:

> The university graduate has been schooled for selective service among the rich of the world. . . . Schools select for each successive level those who have, at earlier stages in the game, proved themselves good risks for the established order. Having a monopoly on both the resources for learning and the investiture of social roles, the university co-opts the discoverer and the potential dissenter. (49)

Despite such moments of co-optation, however, there are also possibilities for dissidence presented in the university setting. Although, as Illich cautions, there are serious limitations here as well:

> There is no question that at present the university offers a unique combination of circumstances which allows some of its members to criticize the whole of society. It provides time, mobility, access to peers and information, and a certain impunity—privileges not equally available to other segments of the population. But the university provides this freedom only to those who have already been deeply initiated into the consumer society and into the need for some kind of obligatory public schooling. (54)

It should be noted that Illich's counsel has often been adopted by anarchist theoreticians and practitioners as a jumping off point for conceptualizing an educational system that is not reliant upon privilege, hierarchy, and co-optation. While to many the concept of anarchy has obvious negative connotations, it is also one of society's most poorly understood systems of thought. Unlike the general perception, most anarchists do not embrace violence as a means of promoting social change (Herbert Read notes, "Peace is anarchy, government is force"(121)); nor are most anarchists categorically opposed to laws, authorities, or social structures—instead reserving their critical energies for *illegitimate* exercises of law, authority, or structure. The difference is crucial in that it opens a space for consideration of some of the more radical suggestions regarding educational alternatives, freed from the unhelpful baggage of political stigma.

At the outset, there exists an impressive and extensive anarchist critique of formal, compulsory education, deftly summarized by Peter Kropotkin's insight that "we are so perverted by an education which from infancy seeks to kill in us the spirit of revolt." Kroptkin also points out the submission to authority that develops, allowing the regulation of every life event from birth through education, friendship and even love. "If this state of things continues," he writes, "we shall lose all initiative, all habit of thinking for ourselves" (197).

Echoing Kropotkin's thoughts and sentiments, Colin Ward similarly laments:

> Ultimately the social function of education is to perpetuate society: it is the socializing function. Society guarantees its future by rearing its children in its own image. . . . The educational system is the largest instrument in the modern state for telling people what to do. . . . Compulsory education is bound up historically, not only with the printing press, the rise of Protestantism and capitalism, but with the growth of the idea of the nation itself. . . . It is in the nature of public authorities to run coercive and hierarchical institutions whose ultimate function is to perpetuate social inequality and to brainwash the young into the acceptance of their particular slot in the organized system. (80)

Nevertheless, in keeping with the notion that anarchism rejects only *illegitimate* structures and not structure per se, Ward goes on to note that Michael Bakunin, in a classically cryptic footnote in the landmark tome *God and the State*, inquires during the late 19th century: "Must we, then, eliminate from society all instruction and abolish all schools? Far from it!" (qtd. in Ward 82). Instead, Bakunin envisions the creation of "schools of human emancipation":

> From these schools will be absolutely eliminated the smallest applications or manifestations of the principle of authority. They will be schools no longer; they will be popular academies, in which neither pupils nor masters will be known, where the people will come

freely to get, if they need it, free instruction, and in
which, rich in their own experience, they will teach in
their turn many things to the professors who shall bring
them knowledge which they lack. This, then, will be a
mutual instruction, an act of intellectual fraternity
between the educated youth and the people. (41)

In this sense, as Ward infers, "the anarchist approach to education
is grounded, not in a contempt for learning, but in a respect for the
learner" (85).

Indeed, the anarchist vision has always contemplated that "the pupil
must be trusted to determine his [or her] own curriculum" (Krimerman
310). In attempting to depict how such a nascent community of scholars
might function, Paul Goodman develops a working model in which a few
professors actually secede from a school to create their own, unchartered
university. "With individual classes of about fifteen . . . the students and
teachers create a small university where they can associate in the
traditional way, but entirely dispensing with the external control,
administration, and bureaucratic machinery . . . that have swamped our
communities of scholars" (453). Herbert Read's essay, "Art As the Basis
of Libertarian Education," is a corollary call for an "education of the
aesthetic sensibility" (408). In it, Read assesses the qualities that the
good teacher in such a setting ought to embody:

He [or she] will try to establish a relationship of
reciprocity and trust between himself and his pupil, and
one of cooperation and mutual aid between all the
individuals within his care [so that] the group develops
spontaneously a social life and cohesion which is
independent of the teacher. We can aim at making our
teachers the friends rather than the masters of their
pupils; as teachers they will not lay down ready-made
rules, but will encourage their children to carry out
their own cooperative activities, and thus spontaneously
to elaborate their own rules. The teacher must be
primarily a person and not a pedagogue, a friend rather
than a master or mistress, an infinitely patient
collaborator. (410)

It thus becomes apparent that, in addition to the quest to secure
individual autonomy, it is similarly the case that higher education in the
anarchist lexicon "is ideally based upon a long and laudable tradition of
autonomous, 'anarchically self-regulating' communities" (Krimerman

449). In other words, just as individual pupils will learn to be self-regulating, so too will the schools they create. Further, as the image comes into even sharper focus, it is imagined in PM's utopian book *Bolo'bolo* that over time "learning and teaching will become an integrated element of life itself . . . . Everybody will be a student and a teacher at the same time. The transmission of wisdom, know-how, theories, and styles will always accompany all productive or reflective processes" (122). In this manner, "a kind of school system can be organized," one that "will be completely voluntary" and for which "there will be no standardization of school systems, no official programs" (123).

In all of these visions there is a penchant for processes that are voluntary, nonhierarchical, self-directed, informal, open-ended, and spontaneous. At the end is a form of *schooling* that transcends any particular meeting time or classroom setting, instead conceiving *education* as part of the everyday experience of life itself, as a mutually-supportive and socially-reflective set of conditions that enables harmony at all levels of the system. All of this harks back to Ivan Illich's assertion that "the inverse of school is possible," and to his related hopes that "we can depend on self-motivated learning instead of employing teachers to bribe or compel the student to find the time and the will to learn" and that "we can provide the learner with new links to the world instead of continuing to funnel all educational programs through the teacher" (104). In many respects, this is a decidedly anarchistic approach to learning, since anarchism has always sought to let "a thousand flowers bloom" rather than impose a specific blueprint for social change (Foer 22). As Ralph Waldo Emerson once plaintively observed: "I have been writing and speaking what were once called novelties for 25 or 30 years, and have not now one disciple. . . . This is my boast, that I have no school or follower. I should account it a measure of the impurity of insight, if it did not create independence" (562).

Actions: Problem-posing, Peacemaking, and Participating

Picking up on these themes and challenges, many contemporary proponents of experiential education have sought to construct practical visions of a "liberatory pedagogy" that avoids the pitfalls identified by Illich and others (Adams 38). Larry Fisk, working from the premise that the nature of education is often "anti-dialogical [and] breeds dependency, subservience or identification with those who already hold power," calls for a problem-posing education that begins with a self-critical "awareness of one's own oppressed or flawed consciousness and conditioning" (177).

To cope with such realities, Fisk posits a peace education that fosters "moral intelligence and peacemaking skills" and that can "provide a holistic climate within which the sense of powerlessness or fatalism can be challenged" (161). Focusing upon familiar themes such as process, critical thinking, and self-discipline, the problem-posing nature of peace education "erodes dependency and fatalism by allowing us to see and experience the world as problematic, unfinished, and exposed to the change which we can help bring about" (177). Specifically, Fisk calls for an educational paradigm in which "people learn values and attitudes which move them to act effectively in particular ways: against war, for environmental protection, for disarmament," and that "actively promotes justice, conflict resolution, service-training, and non-violent action" (180). Such sentiments mirror Illich's insights from a generation earlier:

> . . .a desirable future depends on our deliberately choosing a life of action over a life of consumption, on our engendering a life style which will enable us to be spontaneous, independent, yet related to each other, rather than maintaining a life style which only allows us to make and unmake, produce and consume—a style of life which is merely a way station on the road to the depletion and pollution of the environment. (75)

Practical manifestations of this call to action appear under a number of pedagogical rubrics. Maurianne Adams' investigation and analysis of social justice education, for example, identifies "action research," "experiential education," "reflective experience," "consciousness raising," and "interactive learning" as distinct but related components of a critical pedagogy (32). Arranging classroom seating in circles instead of rows, breaking classes down into small working groups, and promoting images of co-learners and co-teachers are all integral to the central aim of maintaining "equitable and reciprocal teacher-student relations within which student expertise is highlighted" and where "students are partly responsible for each others' academic success" (Adams 34). In this sense, as Fisk observes, it might be said that students become teachers and teachers become students (176). This observation parallels Paulo Freire's admonition that "education must begin with the solution of the teacher-student contradiction, by reconciling the poles of the contradiction so that both are simultaneously teachers and students" (122).

Especially important in this regard is the re-invention of the teacher as *facilitator*, a role which calls for attributes such as "support, passion, awareness, knowledge, and skills," and often "requires the teacher to do a

lot of thinking on her feet" (Griffin 279). Hence, a facilitator can play
many roles: *participant*, in which "the facilitator can comfortably talk
with students about her own experiences, feelings, and struggles;" *guide*,
which encompasses "the ability to pose questions, raise contradictions,
encourage and model self-reflection, and summarize group discussions;"
teacher, for times when "information needs to be presented to students;"
and *activist*, when it becomes "appropriate to encourage students to act
on their beliefs" (284). In each case, the overarching aim is to create a
classroom environment that will "balance the emotional and cognitive
components of the learning process . . . acknowledge and support the
personal while illuminating the systemic . . . attend to social relations
within the classroom . . . [and] utilize reflection and experience as tools
for student-centered learning" (Adams 42). Applied in the classroom,
these directives can serve to foster educational experiences that promote
individual participation, collective solidarity, and a consciousness
grounded in the pursuit of peace and justice.

Evaluation: From Classroom to Community

In having had the unique opportunity to facilitate courses at Prescott
College (including Peace Studies, Human Rights, and Social
Movements), I am guided by such teachings and insights. For instance,
during the build-up to and aftermath of the recent wars with Afghanistan
and Iraq, I sought to strike a balance in the classroom between critical
inquiries into the background and nature of the conflicts, students'
emotional concerns and intellectual responses, and my own commitment
to practices of non-violent direct action and civil disobedience. As events
unfolded, often at a rapid pace and with a sense of increasing complexity
and historical foreboding, it became apparent that whatever else we did
in the classroom it was bound to touch upon the issues of the day. In
fact, I often would set aside significant time at the beginning of each class
for a discussion of current events, including asking students to share news
articles they had read or stories of events such as rallies or teach-ins in
which they had participated. At times when world events would reach a
particular crisis point, it was not unusual to spend nearly an entire class
session on current issues and concerns. In so doing, students often
expressed gratitude for the opportunity, noting that in some of their other
courses such subjects were avoided altogether. I must admit that while it
was difficult at times to work through my own feelings and concerns
openly and on a daily basis in this fashion, there is no doubt that my
comprehension of the issues and sense of positive possibilities was greatly

enhanced through this regular access to the students' inquiries, insights, and perceptions.

On another level, I found that these times presented enormous opportunities for students to participate in specific activities that greatly enhanced the academic experience. Our excursions included peace rallies and anti-war demonstrations (both locally and across the state), visits from social justice advocates such as Voices in the Wilderness (who brought back eyewitness reports from Iraq) and Starhawk (who spoke on Permaculture & Activism), and trips to teach-ins and conferences around the region—including a particularly memorable visit to Berkeley where students participated in panel discussions and decision-making forums with hundreds of others from across the western United States. In each case, the students were able to decide on their own level of participation (including the option to opt out altogether, a choice with no prejudice attached), and often acquired important insights into not only the substance of issues such as human rights or social movements, but into the practice of such concepts as well. Moreover, these experiences raised numerous opportunities for dialogue (such as why a particular sign slogan was adopted or how a march route was chosen), a plethora of teachable moments (such as what worked and what didn't in the student decision-making forum at Berkeley), and (not to be overlooked) a chance to actually have plain old fun in times of great strife and tension.

Looking back, I can absolutely report that both in the classroom and during outside activities, the prevailing mood was one of optimism and hopefulness. The truly remarkable fact is that none of us would likely have been able to sustain such energies on our own; but through the experience of coming together regularly and exercising our minds and emotional centers, we were able to help each other make sense of unfolding events and maintain a spirit of empowerment in the face of increasing fear, repression, and violence. My own observations and feedback from the students suggests that a large measure of our collective positive experience was due to the open-ended and non-hierarchical nature of the classroom environment, as well as to the feeling of being in a safe space to explore such issues that seemed to derive from my own willingness to voice concerns, to elaborate upon fears and doubts, or to discuss political activities. In our ongoing, mutually respectful dialogues, the teacher-student contradiction that Freire warns against often solved itself as we would share perceptions and discuss readings not as social role-players, but simply as people searching for compassion and understanding in difficult times. Ultimately, then, the deepest sense of evaluation I am able to offer is that we retained our sense of being people (in both the individual and collective senses of the word) even as the world seemed to plunge further into chaos and violence. Indeed, it is no small irony that it may, in fact, have been our implicit classroom anarchy that brought about a feeling of order and peace and that helped us, both students and teacher alike, to maintain a spirit of hopefulness about the future.

Putting all of this together, a picture begins to emerge in which teaching methods, student experiences, and social change are overlapping and mutually reinforcing constructs. In a strong sense, young people represent the cutting edge of peace action, and it is through cultivating their sense of rebellious energy that the emancipatory potential of education is most readily realized. Further, the individuals that emerge from such settings are likely to be hopeful and not full of despair and disaffection; action-oriented and not apathetic; dissident and not conformist; community-minded and not ego-centric. Building a better world would seem to be off to a good start if just this much could be accomplished in our educational milieus. In a world of militarism, violence, and uncertainty, it may even be the case that the need for a critical pedagogy for peace has never been greater.

Still, the first step in any struggle may be the belief that positive change is possible, no matter the apparent length of the odds one is facing. As Aldous Huxley observes in issuing his call for an "education for freedom" in *Brave New World Revisited*: "Perhaps the forces that now menace freedom are too strong to be resisted for very long. It is still our duty to do whatever we can to resist them" (174). If there is a single overarching principle guiding a pedagogy premised on experience and participation, it may be this notion that each and every one of us has the power, ability, and responsibility to work for a better today, in the hope of realizing an even brighter tomorrow.

Works Cited

Adams, Maurianne. 1997. "Pedagogical Frameworks for Social Justice Education." *Teaching for Diversity and Social Justice: A Sourcebook*. Ed. Maurianne Adams, Lee Anne Bell, and Pat Griffin. New York: Routledge, 1997. 30-43.

Bakunin, Michael. *God and the State*. New York: Dover, 1970. Barash, David P., ed. *Approaches to Peace: A Reader in Peace Studies*. New York: Oxford, 2000.

Emerson, Ralph Waldo. *Selected Prose and Poetry*. 2nd ed. New York: Holt, Rinehart and Winston, 1969.

Fisk, Larry J. "Shaping Visionaries: Nurturing Peace Through Education." *Patterns of Conflict, Paths to Peace*. Ed. Larry

J. Fisk and John L. Schellenberg. New York: Broadview, 2000. 159-93. Foer, Franklin. "Protest Too Much." *The New Republic* May 2000: 21-23.

Freire, Paulo. *The Pedagogy of the Oppressed*. New York: Continuum, 1970.

Goodman, Paul. "Anarchism and the Ideal University." *Patterns of Anarchy: A Collection of Writings on the Anarchist Tradition*. Ed. Leonard I. Krimerman and Lewis Perry. New York: Anchor, 1966. 449-56.

Griffin, Pat. "Facilitating Social Justice Education Courses." *Teaching for Diversity and Social Justice: A Sourcebook*. Ed. Maurianne Adams, Lee Anne Bell, and Pat Griffin. New York: Routledge, 1997. 279-98.

Huxley, Aldous. *Brave New World Revisited*. New York: Harper & Row, 1958.

Illich, Ivan. *Deschooling Society*. New York: Harrow, 1972.

Krimerman, Leonard I., and Lewis Perry, eds. *Patterns of Anarchy: A Collection of Writings on the Anarchist Tradition*. New York: Anchor, 1966.

Kropotkin, Peter. *Kropotkin's Revolutionary Pamphlets*. New York: Benjamin Blom, 1968.

P.M. *Bolo'bolo*. Brooklyn: Semiotext(e), 1995.

Read, Herbert. "Art as the Basis of Libertarian Education." *Patterns of Anarchy: A Collection of Writings on the Anarchist Tradition*. Ed. Leonard I. Krimerman and Lewis Perry.

New York: Anchor, 1966. 406-12.

—. "The Prerequisite of Peace." *Anarchy and Order: Essays in Politics.* Boston: Beacon, 1971. 109-21.

Ward, Colin. *Anarchy in Action.* New York: Harper, 1973.

Samuel N. Henrie, Ph.D.

In setting out to write this essay, Samuel Henrie had in mind the person who does not already have experience with, or theoretical knowledge about, experiential education. He also kept in mind the more traditional educator who may not see how experiential education can be applied somewhere besides the lab or the field.

"Many books and articles on this topic deal with outdoor education,"
Henrie says, "but I fervently believe that experiential education is equally applicable to traditional subjects and the classroom setting."

Samuel Henrie began his teaching career at Emery Junior-Senior High School in the San Francisco Bay area. He is the author of Writings of John D. Lee *and the English translator of Peruvian author, J.A. Bravo's novel,* To Melisa Eloísa*. A former Senior Program Associate at Far West Laboratory for Educational Research and Development in San Francisco, he is now faculty emeritus at Prescott College, where he has been teaching since 1971.*

Experiential Education in the Academic Classroom

I.

"I am a bit worried about your having to fill in for Les," the Vice Principal told me, "since you're new to teaching." He had called me to his office at the beginning of my morning prep period because, seven weeks into the term, Lester Lawson had suddenly taken ill. They needed someone to take over his seventh grade science class for a few weeks. The class met last period, late afternoon, when I had a second prep hour. New teachers were often given more prep time, and I was teaching on a provisional credential. Science wasn't my major, but I had completed several science courses for my B.A. and, more importantly, I was the only teacher available last period.

"I think I can handle it," I assured the Vice Principal.

"They're using the state approved textbook, but Les couldn't do much with the kids," he said. "They're about four lessons behind."

I had already looked through the textbook, *The World Of Science Today*, and it was about four *decades* behind, the cover featuring a faded picture of two children awkwardly bending over a lab table. Their eyes were blue, and they had test tubes in their hands. Our school was fully integrated (out of necessity not good will): black, white, tan, yellow, and poor.

"Do I have to use the book?"

"It's the state-approved curriculum," he said, "but considering the circumstances you can have some latitude, so long as you cover the same material. What do you have in mind?"

"Some lab work."

"Class demonstrations?" he said.

"Well, no," I said. "I was hoping to have the kids do some experiments."

"We don't do that here," he said with a straight face, "except in the eleventh grade chemistry course. And they do cut up flowers and one frog in tenth grade biology."

"You said I could have some latitude," I reminded him. "But believe me, I won't do anything expensive or dangerous."

"Expensive?"

"I'll need a small budget," I said. Then I broached my real concern. "How is Les doing? What happened?"

The Vice Principal hesitated, studying the new blotter on the top of his desk. Looking up, he said, "Nervous problems." Realizing that was not an adequate response, he added, "He's been hospitalized—a kind of breakdown. We're not sure how long he'll be gone."

He ended our meeting with a caution: "These are seventh graders— and they're not like the high schoolers you're teaching now. Establish tight discipline right away." He hesitated, then said, "Watch out for Ruben. If he gets the idea you're vulnerable, he'll take advantage."

At a meeting later in the day, before I had stepped in to my new assignment, I asked the Vice Principal who this Ruben kid was. He took me into his office, unlocked a drawer, and pulled out a file. He pointed with his pencil lead to the number 84 on one of the pages. "Ruben's I.Q."

I still didn't get it.

"Well, what can you expect from Ruben? He doesn't learn, and he gets bored, so he's the class clown and he sets them all off. Lucky for you he ditches science class a lot and goes home early." He smiled, and added, "By the way, Ruben has his virtues too; he's a good athlete."

The next day I met the class for the first time. I imagined they were eyeing me coldly and saying to themselves, "I wonder how long *this* geek will last?" I had decided to limit myself only to questions, to see if I could get them to open up and tell me what they really wanted to learn. "What have you been doing in class so far?"

No one spoke.

I held up the book, and a general groan arose. "Pretty boring, huh?"

A giggle rippled across the class. I ceremoniously dropped the book in the wastebasket and they straightened in their desks. Every eye was fixed on me. But then I retrieved the book, and they went limp again. "Can't do that yet," I said. "Okay if we have a little test, just to see where we are?"

"No," an anonymous voice barked from the back of the room.

I purposely didn't react. "The first chapter is about electricity. Can anyone tell me what a circuit is?" A girl with Chinese features raised her hand timidly. My scholar, I thought. "Tell me your name before you answer the question," I said. Her face flushed and she turned away.

"She's Lynn," came another voice from the back.

"Lynn," I smiled. "Tell us what an electrical circuit is."

"What happened to Mr. Lawson?" she asked.

"He had a heart attack," a voice answered. "We gave it to him," chimed in another. "Shut up!" someone yelled. "We didn't do it; he's just old." "My aunt had a heart attack, and she died," yet another voice rang out.

Lynn stood up, distressed, and looked around the class distressfully. "Did Mr. Lawson die?"

Just then, the door opened and the Vice Principal's head popped in. He'd probably been listening at the door. "How are things going?"

Relieved, I invited him in. "The class would like to know how Mr. Lawson is doing."

They started peppering him with questions, and I was happy to let him take over. He spent the rest of the hour soothing them with white lies: "Mr. Lawson just fainted." "Mr. Lawson didn't have a heart attack, and he is not going to die like Taysha's aunt." "Mr. Lawson was ill before he ever got to school that morning. He should have stayed home, but he likes you students so much." They weren't buying that, bursting into sardonic laughter from the back of the room. He answered all of their questions, telling them Mr. Lawson thought it was awesome to ride in an ambulance and that he would be back, well-rested and ready to go, in a few days.

I had met the enemy (my own lack of imagination), and the first battle had resulted in a humiliating defeat. But I now understood what I was dealing with. Over the weekend I went to a radio parts store and armed myself with a handful of resistors, transistors, a ferrite coil, a set of tuning plates, a role of small-gauge copper wire, ear phones, some shorting clips, a pair of needle-nosed pliers and a 4.5 volt battery—about $18 all told (it was the '60s). Using a diagram from my old Boy Scout manual, I strung together a crystal radio with a one-stage amplifier and taped it to the bottom of a shoebox.

Monday afternoon, while my seventh graders were drifting into the classroom, I was stringing a cable of copper wire between the pencil sharpener and the window latch.

"What're you doing that for Mr. Henrie?" the kids asked.

"You'll see."

As I was about to begin, an athletic young man, almost as tall as I was, entered the classroom. He lightly sprang to the top of the first student's desk in the middle row and danced from desktop to desktop as the kids dodged his feet. Then he plopped into the last desk at the back, smiling happily. "How y'all doin', Mr. Henrie?"

"Ruben, right?"

"Yeah," he said, his eyes fixed on mine.

I returned the challenge. "Guess what I've got in this box, Ruben."

He sauntered up the aisle and looked into the shoebox. "I don't know, some wires and ear pieces and shit."

Everyone was leaning forward to see if I would kick Ruben out, or maybe collapse like Mr. Lawson had. But I calmly attached one end of a wire to the makeshift antenna and fixed the other to a clip in the shoebox. I slipped the battery into its holder and handed Ruben the earphones, which he put on. His grin disappeared as his eyes widened, and he began to say, half-sing, the words of a top-10 rock-n-roll song. By this time, most of the kids were crowding around my desk at the front of the room. "Hey, Ruben, let me hear." "It's my turn." "Come on Rube, we get to hear, too."

Conveniently, the Vice Principal poked his head in again. "Everything Okay?" he asked, alarmed at seeing animated kids singing and crowding around me.

"Just right," I said.

He took a second look, then withdrew, closing the door behind him.

After every student had taken a turn with the earphones, I said, "Each one of you can make one of these radios for yourself, but I'm not going to tell you about it until everyone is in a seat and you've quieted down."

They went back to their desks, and Ruben sat in the front row.

"Okay, now, here's what we can do. We can forget about these books and learn the same stuff by doing things. And we'll start with radios if that's okay with you."

"Yeah." "Cool." "Groovy!" (This was the '60s.)

But there was a catch. I said they would first have to pass a test on electromagnetism and radio, and they would also have to write a three-page paper. This, of course, was not cool to them, and they were immediately suspicious. "That's the deal," I said. "Take it or leave it. But don't worry, I'll help you and you can help each other."

They talked it over for a few minutes and then warily accepted. I didn't approve the deal—the contract—until everyone held up a hand to agree, even Ruben.

After class I went to the Vice Principal's office. He also approved and said I could have $12 for each student to purchase parts. I wanted them to commit, however, so I decided they should pay at least $5 dollars each and the school could finance the rest.

Wednesday, in class, I handed out a circuit diagram, giving proper credit to the Boy Scout Manual of 1952. Then I showed them every component of the shoebox, told of its function and how it corresponded to a symbol on the circuit diagram.

"Oh, we'll never get this," someone said. "Yes we will," others encouraged.

Undaunted, I sprang the $5 charge on the students and some of them rebelled: "I don't have no five bucks," one said. "It isn't fair," said another. "Hey," a particularly sharp student observed, "school's supposed to be free."

"Well, school *is* free. You're not paying me, or paying to rent the classroom. But this will be *your* radio. It will belong to you; so you should help buy the parts. That's fair, and that's the deal," I said. "Otherwise we go back to the books."

They agreed quickly this time. Another decision point and they were still with me.

The class period was half over when I pulled from my desk drawer a completed radio, leads soldered, mounted on a 6"x 6" piece of plywood. It was my radio. The kids were awestruck. I strung up the antenna again and let them listen, one at a time. The bell rang, but they wouldn't leave. Everyone had to listen, and then they listened again. A few of them stuck around until 4:30, chattering excitedly about their own radios and how they would decorate them. The janitor finally kicked us out so he could clean, frowning at the wire strung across the front of the room and muttering, "What the hell is this?"

"Science class," I said and took it down.

Within a month, all of my students had passed the test, written original papers, and built beautiful individualized radios to which they gave pet names. They learned to tune in most of the local stations. They didn't just listen to popular music; some would listen to the news broadcasts and tell me about what they'd heard. Without my prompting, they began to experiment with antennas, stringing wires across the roof of the school (with the help of the janitor) and their own homes and apartment buildings.

One day, one of the girls approached me, her eyes glowing with excitement, to tell me that she had discovered that the finger stop on a rotary dial telephone made a terrific antenna. Others discovered that water pipes and fire escapes would work. A thin boy named Edward Gibb, who usually slumped quietly in his desk as though trying to disappear, accidentally bridged a resistor across two wires in a manner different from the diagram. The reception trebled in volume. The next Monday, I passed out an improved version of the Boy Scout diagram, now labeled *The Edward Gibb Circuit*. From that day, Edward was a changed young man, and I have often wondered if his little error launched a career in electronics.

Building on a foundation of real experience, these kids—supposedly unable to compete with kids from suburban schools—were able to learn science principles and systems much more sophisticated than those in the state textbook. They came to understand the electromagnetic spectrum and how it propagates in wavelengths as small as x-rays and as long as radio waves. They could explain how light is similar to radio, both being made of waves of photons that travel very fast. They speculated about how radio waves can pass through walls. They gained a basic understanding of how electric currents could be converted to energy fields and vice versa. They eventually got a very difficult concept—how carrier waves are rectified in a diode, and that signal is amplified by a triode. As part of the test they had to pass before they could buy their components, they explained, at a basic level, what each component of the little radio did to convert radio waves emanating through the air into the music and talk they could hear through their ear phones. We visited a local broadcasting facility where they saw the transmitter tower that was casting radio AM carrier waves in every direction. For their three-page research papers, they took topics ranging from Marconi to the invention of the transistor.

Mr. Lawson did not return to the school. I taught seventh-grade science for the rest of that year and continued to teach it for three more years as a part of my regular assignment. The students and I raised insects, recording their development from egg to adult and to egg again, logging changes in weight and length in good scientific form. We counted the four moons orbiting Jupiter that were visible through good binoculars, tracking changes in their positions over a month, in the process repeating some of the discoveries of Copernicus and Galileo. On the football field, we laid out a scale model of the sun, earth, and moon, using a beach ball, a golf ball and a marble, and the kids could explain the structure of the solar system, phases of the moon, and how our Earth's daily rotation and yearly orbit create the days and seasons. We raised cultures of bacteria in petri dishes that we had prepared and sterilized ourselves using a pressure cooker. One girl tested antibiotics and antiseptic mouthwashes on cultures grown from scrapings of her own teeth.

These kids in an inner-city school were not just passively enduring science lessons; they were becoming scientists. They were teaching me how to become an experiential teacher.

Since then, some forty years ago, I have taught at the university and post-graduate level, and consulted in the development of elementary school programs. But the principles, and even the methods, I learned from inner-city seventh graders have been applicable in every case, with every population, and at every level I have taught.

II.

I began this essay with a simple human story to give my readers an *experience*, albeit that experience was vicarious. To have begun with theory would have contradicted the point I wished to make. First a teacher must appeal to the whole person, grasp the learner's attention by appealing to something that is real to the learner. That creates a learning theater that can be filled with the joy of discovery, rather than the pall of coercions, boredom and resentment. There is plenty of time later for analysis, categorization, and focus on technically right answers. I trust we can all relate to the struggles of seventh graders to grow up and establish themselves as individuals in the world.

Some educators may believe that experiential learning can only occur in the laboratory or in a field setting. The error in that thinking has to do with a misunderstanding of what experiential learning is all about. It has nothing to do with the setting, and everything to do with the process. While experiential educators have described the process in a variety of terminologies, there are common elements that span the whole curriculum, from rock climbing to agriculture, from creative writing to philosophy. As a professor of philosophy, my approach, expressed in my own terminology, employs the following principles:

1. Base your design of the opening phase upon the learner's previous experiences, fund of knowledge, learning capability and style, and motivation. Do not begin with the abstracted hierarchy of facts and theories that is the usual starting point in any traditional subject matter.

2. Address as many of the learner's senses as possible, so that learning is not flat, one-dimensional and abstract. A river not only carries water, it also smells and has a feel. It's alive in a way no one-dimensional description of it could be. In like fashion, a philosophical theory has a look and a feel that can be brought to the learner's senses through paintings of the period, music, stories, etc. Students have convinced me that their lives are living philosophy, and they confront the great question in their own terms nearly every day.

3. Allow the student to learn through a modality that matches his or her capacity, to the extent that is possible. I don't believe in the validity of IQ, but Ruben's capacity for learning and growth turned out to be well above the number 84.

4. Conceive of the teacher's role as predominantly that of an architect of the learning system/process, not as the authority and arbiter of truth, or the principal fount of information. An experiential classroom is student-centered, not teacher-centered. Another important aspect of the teacher's role is to supply support and positive feedback to the students. Learning is an emotion-based process as much as it is intellectual, and at any age the student needs to feel successful and appreciated. A rule I learned from the seventh grade students is this: Don't reject a student's answer or statement by saying, "You're wrong." It is the teacher's job to see what is *right* about the student's reasoning and to build on that. The classroom is not an arena to display who is smartest, teacher or student, but an environment in which all cooperate for a higher purpose.

5. Encourage *discovery* of knowledge, rather than memorization of facts and principles to be later regurgitated on tests and in papers. The student should be learning how to take initiative and organize a learning process, not just a catalogue of facts and theories. I hasten to add that there is a very important phase in which classification

systems are used, facts and principles are learned *within an experiential context*, and learning should be verified (tested). Experiential learning is at least as rigorous as conventional approaches. It is not fuzzy-minded, devoid of intellectual content, or uncritical.

6. Knowledge is not fully learned until it is applied to as many problems, issues, and projects as possible. Real learning is not just to fulfill empty requirements and pass tests. After college, one is seldom asked to take a test, and almost never simply to prove one's learning. The classroom learning sequence should also be seen as a model for gaining and using new knowledge throughout life.

7. In the highest sense, all learning is ethical and aesthetic. This is another way of saying that the material that is learned should have real meaning for the students. It should enhance their mental life and behavior.

To conclude, I think it appropriate to share some methodological tools that work when I teach philosophy and, therefore, should work equally as well in a variety of other abstract, and not-so-abstract, subjects:

Story Telling: both the instructor's and students' stories.

Theater: adapt texts, like scenes from Plato's dialogues, and act out the parts before the class.

Thought Experiments: which can be either created as issues arise in the class or presented orally by students from their portfolio notes.

Model Building: creating and elaborating intellectual structures and critiquing them in class.

Debate: particularly effective in helping students see the ethical implications of ideas.

Philosophy Conferences: students write original five-minute papers and present them in a formal conference conducted in class or a presentation hall (attended by guests if possible) with each reading followed by a formal critique.

Question Log: focusing on students asking good questions rather than reiterating facts.

Student-Produced Papers As Class Texts: incorporating high quality papers written by students of past years into class readers, also duplicating and handing out papers written by students in the current class.

Contract Learning: meeting with students individually to design and approve their contracts.

Honoring Self-Report: as the philosopher, Michael Schriven, has said, in the humanistic and social realm the most sensitive and accurate evaluation technique is self-report.

I have used all of these and many more experiential techniques to create dynamic philosophy classes. The possibilities are only limited by the teacher's imagination. Experiential education in the academic classroom requires little budget or special equipment and it can be very powerful. Over the years, students—whether they are seventh graders or graduate students—have expressed how much they are stimulated, entertained, edified, challenged, and educated in mind and spirit when experiential learning is used in the academic classroom.

K.L. COOK

With almost disarming honesty, K.L. (Kenny) Cook examines the often baffling, often frustrating, and ultimately rewarding role of the advisor. Though his examples and anecdotes are specific to Prescott College, principles that are universal—such as the advisor's role in framing students' educational journeys or the challenge of combating an educational world that grows more institutional and less personal every year—emerge from the essay.

"My intentions are to show how our advising system, like our teaching philosophy, honors student-centered learning and reinforces experiential and competence-based education. Students aren't just asked to accumulate prescribed courses and credits," he says. "They are required to define, describe, and demonstrate their competence and liberal artistry."

K.L. Cook joined the faculty at Prescott College in 1992 and has served as Associate Dean for the Resident Degree Program (RDP) since 2002. A professor of creative writing and literature, his fiction, essays, articles, poetry, and reviews have appeared in numerous literary magazines, newspapers, and journals, including American Short Fiction, Harvard Review, Threepenny Review, Witness, *and* Shenandoah. *His collection of linked stories,* Last Call *(2004), won the* Prairie Schooner Book Prize for Fiction, *and his novel,* The Girl from Charnelle, *will be published in 2006.*

EVERY STUDENT IS AN HONOR STUDENT: ADVISING AT PRESCOTT COLLEGE

I was not a very good advisor when I began teaching at Prescott College in the fall of 1992. After four years as a visiting instructor at the College of Charleston, where I taught writing and literature but had few official advising responsibilities, I was confident as a teacher but at a loss as an advisor. My first new student advising day had me saddled with twelve new advisees and no real clue about what I was doing. I suffered through that exhausting day in a giddy, incompetent euphoria, apologizing for my ignorance and relying on colleagues to rectify my damage.

All my efforts to serve the college beyond teaching—task forces, committee work, department leadership, and now as associate dean—

have stemmed primarily from my desire to improve advising, which is a huge part of every faculty member's job at Prescott College and an often baffling and frustrating one. I yearned, and still yearn, to be a better advisor. My periodic failures made me want to understand why the college operates the way it does, what intentions are behind our processes, and how those intentions make the educational experience richer, as well as more exhausting. I wanted to have answers for my students' probing and often troubling questions. I wanted to be able to engage in the ongoing debate with my colleagues about underlying educational assumptions and how those assumptions get played out in the practical, day-to-day logistics of advising. Despite my frustrations, I'm grateful to be in an institution that values these examinations, that is open to change, and that is surprisingly nimble in its sensitivity to student needs.

In this essay, I give an overview of the Prescott College (PC) journey, describing and analyzing the underlying assumptions of our advising model—exploring how we operationalize our mission of providing experiential, competence-based liberal arts education. Perhaps the best thing about our advising system is that it requires students to grapple with the meta-cognitive issues of their education. They don't just take classes here or follow a pre-arranged plan of study. Instead, they must *articulate* what it means to be competent in a field of study, what it means to have breadth of knowledge, and what it means to be a liberally educated citizen of the world. This kind of approach to undergraduate education is, I believe, genuinely radical in an educational world that is growing more institutional and less personal every year.

Overview of the PC Advising Process

Since its inception in the mid-sixties, Prescott College has prided itself on its strong advisor/advisee relationships. One of the great things about teaching and advising at Prescott College is that most students come here because they want to. They haven't been forced to enroll here. In fact, in most cases, students have had to search out Prescott College and convince their parents that this is the place for them. Many of our students apply here after experimenting with higher education at other, usually more traditional, institutions. This is the place where they believe they can flourish, where they will find themselves integral to any class, where their voices will be heard not only in the classroom or field but also in the design and implementation of their academic careers. As advisors, we are here to support them in their endeavors, to clarify their options, and to help them see their personal aspirations and goals within a larger context—academic, personal, ecological, artistic, service-related, and global. We want to help our students be agents of positive change in the world.

Our educational philosophy emphasizes individualized attention, and our graduation process is not designed primarily for efficiency in the way more traditional college and university processes are. One of the central roles of the advisor is to constantly frame and reframe the Prescott College journey for students. They read about it in their handbooks. They hear about it during Wilderness Orientation. Yet, like any journey, the questions and issues and subtleties will only be urgent as students encounter the obstacles and opportunities strewn along their paths.

While theoretically every student's journey is unique, all students must deal with common issues. It's important that they understand that Prescott College is, first and foremost, "for the liberal arts and the environment." Everything we do and plan and dream is embodied in that phrase. We are not a vocational school. We believe that the best stewards of the earth and the most effective agents of change are liberally educated citizens. We expect students to have some experience with and appreciation for various modes of understanding the world: historical, literary, artistic, scientific, social, physical, and spiritual. We expect them to cultivate political, cultural, and ecological awareness, as well as communication and mathematical skills. We also believe that a liberal arts education emphasizes process as much as content. At its best, experiential learning animates theory and engages the whole person.

We are also a competence-driven college. Students don't just accumulate credits, get their tickets punched, and graduate. Students are expected to be literate in their fields of study, to have mastered the methodologies of a discipline, to have applied and integrated and personalized their learning, and to have demonstrated competence through the design and execution of a senior project. We want them to define, describe, and demonstrate how their particular courses, independent studies, and experiences create a coherent academic plan. We believe that every student is an honor student and that the demonstration of competence requires a capstone experience. We believe that an Individualized Graduation Committee—a team consisting of the student, the advisor, a second faculty member, and a fellow student—helps students clarify and achieve their personal aspirations. We want students to grapple with the larger philosophical issues of their education.

Self-Direction

In *The RDP Student Handbook*, self-direction, another cornerstone of our pedagogy, is defined this way:

> At Prescott College, self-direction is considered the manifestation of motivation, the ability to direct oneself (but not to the exclusion of involvement with other people), self-knowledge, and a willingness to ask for help when necessary. A self-directed person demonstrates the ability to set goals and objectives, take individual responsibility, initiate and carry out projects with little or no outside inducement, and form value judgments independently.

We often assume that our students already should be self-directed learners when they begin college. This is a fallacy. While many of our students are self-directed by nature, they often need coaching and practical skills in the art of self-direction. As Flannery O'Connor, an American fiction writer, said, "Young artists must cultivate the habit of art." Many of our learning processes and tools—the seminar-style structure of our classrooms, course contracts, learning portfolios, self-evaluations, practicum requirements, independent studies, Degree Plans, Senior Project Applications—help students learn to see themselves as the primary architects of their education and help them not only take advantage of the privileges but also to accept the responsibilities of self-direction. We want them to succeed not only at Prescott College but in life. We want them to see their educational journey, and the tools they use to navigate that journey, as metaphors for navigating the difficult terrain of their post-collegiate careers. We try not to assume, especially with new students, that they have mastered these skills or have cultivated the habit of self-direction. We have to prompt and nudge and find the appropriate teaching moments to bring these lessons home.

Competence, Breadth, & Liberal Arts

At Prescott College, "competence" is our term for major, and "breadth" is our term for minor. Consisting of a minimum of 12-16 courses, a student's competence(s) must address these five qualitative criteria: (1) literacy in the field, (2) mastery of methodology, (3) interconnections between the competence and other areas of study, (4) application of learning, and (5) personalization of learning. Consisting of 6-8 courses, a student's breadth(s) also addresses these five criteria but in less depth than a competence.

Most liberal arts colleges and universities are descended from the Greek system of education that espoused the study of the *Trivium* (grammar, rhetoric, and logic) and the *Quadrivium* (geometry, arithmetic, music, and astronomy). The modern incarnation of the Greek system consists of three main branches of knowledge: the humanities (literature, history, the arts, and languages), the social sciences (psychology, sociology, anthropology, economics, etc.), and the physical and biological sciences (including mathematics). This approach to the liberal arts is content-centered, and most liberal arts colleges satisfy their liberal arts imperatives through general education requirements—what our dean, Gret Antilla, likes to call "The Noah's Ark Model of Education." In other words, you become a liberally educated student by loading up your cognitive ark with two of everything: two composition and literature courses, two language courses, two physical science courses (and two labs), two history courses, two social science courses, two arts courses, two math courses, and two physical education courses.

An alternative to this content-based approach is the concentration on the skills needed of a liberally educated student—for example, environmental awareness, aesthetic appreciation, critical thinking, ethical valuing, communication, and multi-cultural awareness. This is the approach that our Adult Degree Program (ADP)—the distance-learning program at Prescott College—has adopted. All students are required to demonstrate these six skills in their overall plan of study. In the Resident Degree Program (RDP), for which I teach, the faculty has adopted this definition of the liberal arts to help guide our students:

> Prescott College is a four-year Liberal Arts College
> striving to prepare students to be life-long learners and
> critical thinkers in a broad, interwoven range of models
> of inquiry: *literary, scientific, artistic, social, spiritual,
> and physical.* We emphasize the interdisciplinary
> connections rather than the distinctions between these
> ways of understanding the world. We are unique in our
> approach to the Liberal Arts in that we emphasize
> direct experience; the process of learning is just as
> important as the content.

In both the ADP and RDP, we believe that the liberal arts should be fostered in *every* course students take, just as the criteria for competence—literacy, methodology, application, interconnection, and personalization—should be guiding principles of each class. This means that Prescott College has only a limited number of core or general education requirements. Students must complete college-level algebra or higher and must meet rigorous writing-across-the-curriculum requirements to demonstrate critical writing and research skills. Other than that, students must work closely with their Individual Graduation Committees to make sure that they do indeed have a well-rounded liberal arts education, and that they are able to articulate the components and benefits of that education.

Conservatory vs. Liberal Arts Approaches to Education

Prescott College is uniquely positioned between conservatory and traditional liberal arts approaches to education. In a conservatory school (MIT or Julliard, for instance), the student spends four years focusing in great depth, and almost exclusively, on a single discipline. The liberal arts tradition emphasizes breadth over depth. The required course work at a liberal arts school is often divided into thirds: 1/3 on general education requirements, 1/3 on the major, and 1/3 on minors and electives.

At Prescott College, because we have a dual mission of both liberal arts and competence-based education, we try to honor students' desires to lean toward greater breadth or greater depth. We have unique graduation formats that allow students to break down their course work in roughly this 1/3, 1/3, 1/3 ratio, or they can strengthen their competence area(s) considerably so that one-half to sometimes two-thirds of their course work is devoted to the competence area and the remaining devoted to liberal arts and additional breadth work. If a student chooses to pursue this second model (which is the norm at Prescott College), they still must demonstrate liberal arts breadth of knowledge in both their Degree Plan and Senior Project Application narratives, which are the two major documents that help students plan and articulate their educational journeys.

Mapping the Journey: The Degree Plan

The Degree Plan is the academic map of the journey. Due three enrollment periods (about eighteen months) before the student intends to graduate, it includes an overview of courses and credits earned, brief descriptions of competence, breadth, and liberal arts areas, lists of courses completed and those to be completed, a tentative senior project plan and description, and additional honors or experience that contribute to competence or breadth. An advisor or faculty member should be able to look at this document and see, in a nutshell, an elegant and coherent academic plan for the student's academic journey. It is also a tool for the Individual Graduation Committee (IGC) and the faculty in the program of competence to help students strengthen, deepen, and broaden the scope of studies.

The Degree Plan goes through a rigorous gauntlet of evaluation. Not only must the two primary advisors on the IGC review and approve the plan, but the Dean's Office evaluates it for minimum quantitative standards. Then the plan undergoes a program review. This involves the program coordinator and two additional faculty members scrutinizing the plan and offering detailed suggestions regarding the quality of the competence, breadth, and liberal arts. The student, in consultation with the IGC, then revises based on this additional feedback and resubmits the plan for approval. This process is similar to graduate program reviews, where every student's plan of study is rigorously evaluated not only by a primary advisor but also by an extended faculty committee and potentially by the whole department.

The Degree Plan may (and usually does) undergo additional changes in the student's final three terms. Those changes are noted and approved by the advisor and IGC and ultimately re-evaluated as part of the Senior Project Application.

The Senior Project: Culmination, Bridge, Calling Card, Legacy

Prescott College differs from most other liberal arts colleges in that we require *every* student, not just designated "honor" students, to design and carry out an ambitious senior project. The senior project at PC is both a demonstration of competence and a culmination of the undergraduate experience. It is an extension of the foundation of theory, method, and research that has been prepared by course work, independent studies, practicum and internship experiences, teaching assistantships, and professional work. It is an opportunity for students to dynamically synthesize their learning. This may take the form of an ambitious research project, a collection of original creative work, a curriculum plan and implementation, a studio art exhibition, a performance, a case or field study, or a challenging internship.

Another way of thinking about the senior project is as a bridge between a student's undergraduate career and the work after graduation. The senior project becomes a calling card that proclaims to graduate schools, prospective employers, and the world, "Look, this is what I'm capable of doing." For some students, the senior project is also a way of providing a legacy. Prescott College's Community Supported Agriculture

(CSA) program, our college newspaper, women's resource center, and Water-Based Wilderness Orientation all began as student-directed senior projects; such projects obviously allow us to collaborate with our students in ways usually reserved for graduate-level research projects. As a result, our students are often challenged (and expected) to do graduate-level work. Our students typically perform exceptionally well if they go on to pursue master's or doctoral studies.

Articulating and Defending the Journey: The Senior Project Application

We ask students to write a formal application before they embark on the senior project, which entails not only a detailed description of the project but also the student's reflective analysis of his or her educational journey. Due at the end of the term before students begin their senior projects, The Senior Project Application (SPA) is a lengthy narrative extension of the Degree Plan. Students must demonstrate their competence in their discipline before beginning the senior project by completing a senior project contract, writing a full narrative description of the competence area, writing a narrative description of the senior project, writing a Liberal Arts Statement that interprets their educational journey and justifies the granting of a Bachelor of Arts degree, and, if substantial alterations of the student's academic program have occurred, formally amending the Degree Plan.

The SPA is a multi-draft document that must be approved by the IGC as well as the relevant program coordinator(s). It fulfills three purposes: it is a planning document, much like a thesis prospectus, that the student and the IGC use to design and approve the substance of the senior project; it is the place where students define, defend, and demonstrate their undergraduate education; and it also serves as a special independent study contract for the student to submit for registration.

Student Approaches to the Senior Project Application

As one can imagine, this process is challenging and requires substantial time and effort beyond the student's course work and other requirements for graduation. As advisors, we try to coach students through this process by offering a number of approaches to writing these narratives:

- Getting It. One approach to writing the SPA is to have students think of it as a 1000-2000 word essay or a sequence of related mini-essays they could give their friends and loved ones who don't know much about Prescott College. After reading the SPA, those loved ones should "get" the Prescott College experience. The goal is to prompt students to make the document authentic, an eloquent and coherent reflective essay.

- **SPA as Argument/Defense.** The most common strategy is to have students think of the SPA as an argumentative essay—an opportunity to describe, analyze, and persuade their IGCs, the Prescott College community, and the greater world that their educational journeys demonstrate a liberal arts education and competence in a given field(s) of study. The SPA is offered as proof of competence and readiness to graduate.

- **SPA as Philosophical Inquiry.** A related strategy is to have students think of the SPA as an inquiry into and examination of the nature of competence and liberal arts. What does it mean to be liberally educated? What are liberal arts/skills? What does it mean to have academic breadth? What does it mean to be "competent," and how does that differ from having a major? This approach doesn't preclude argumentation or description or analysis, but it frames the SPA as part of a lifelong philosophical inquiry.

- **SPA as Privilege/Opportunity/Responsibility.** Another contextual framework for the SPA is to have the student consider it as a privilege. Very few colleges or universities *allow* students the opportunity to play a major role in designing and defining their education; most provide a list of required core courses and major and minor requirements. While Prescott College provides advising documents that range from prescriptive to flexible, no two plans will (or should) look the same. We have few core requirements. In exchange for this flexibility and freedom, students must shoulder the responsibility of persuading the college (and the greater academic and professional community) that they are indeed liberally educated and competent. At most other schools, students take the prescribed classes and then graduate. Here, students must make sense of their education and then persuasively articulate and demonstrate it.

Senior Project Description

The Senior Project Description demands that students articulate how their senior project(s) serves as a capstone experience in their competence area(s). It includes a description of the goals and objectives, venues, resources and subjects, specific activities, timeline, evaluation process, bibliography, and other relevant information. It indicates the final form the project will take: thesis paper, research report, article for publication, artistic exhibition or performance, collection of poems or stories, etc. Finally, it demonstrates knowledge in the field of study, skills to apply learning to real-world problems, and personalization of the learning.

Liberal Arts Statement
Students reflect on the broader meaning of their education in the Liberal Arts Statement. Students are asked to assert their own views of the liberal arts, not simply replicate published definitions. They describe how their college program has equipped them with both broad knowledge of the world and specific understanding in their areas of concentration. They discuss the critical thinking skills they now use and the specific skills pertinent to their field(s). They define the ethical issues they have examined and the commitments they have made in such critical areas as the environment, social justice, and global awareness. They explain how the Prescott College emphasis on real-life experience and practical application of knowledge has shaped their learning process. They discuss personal breadth and self-direction, indicating (a) self-awareness and self-understanding; (b) integration of the spiritual, ethical, social, physical, and intellectual aspects of their lives; (c) progress towards realization of their full potential; (d) ethical commitments as seen in personal reflections and ways of relating to others and the environment; and (e) commitment to service.

Competence Description
The competence description can be both the easiest and most difficult part of the SPA to write. It is easier because students understand and are passionate about their competence areas. Yet it is daunting to distill what one has learned in four years into a few pages. Students must define, describe, and document the competence area in a narrative format addressing these five qualitative standards:
- **Literacy in the Field:** a working knowledge of the basic history of the field(s), important individuals and their work, and major theories and their applications as found in key books and articles.
- **Mastery of Methodology:** a demonstrated understanding of, and capacity to use, the research techniques, scholarly methods, leadership skills, artistic modes of expression, etc., that are commonly employed in the field(s).
- **Interconnection of Learning:** an ability to see the relationships among the components of one's education and important ethical

issues of the field which affect the world.

- **Application of Learning:** a demonstrated ability to apply the theories of the field of study to real-world situations and experiential demonstration of learning both in and out of the classroom.
- **Personalization of Learning:** discussion and demonstration of the internalization of work, creative and independent study, and ethical and personal challenges of working in the field.

What follows is an extended example of a competence description for Creative Writing and Literature to illustrate what we expect from our students:

Literacy in the Field

As T.S. Eliot points out, the literary artist must not only write but must also apprentice himself or herself to a long and rich literary tradition. You can't exist in a literary vacuum; no truly original work springs from a void. My literary education has been two-fold: I have attempted to work in many different genres (poetry, fiction, nonfiction, and scriptwriting), and I have supplemented my creative efforts with a rigorous study of literature—in the context of creative writing classes, in more straightforward literature courses, and in interdisciplinary courses. Many of my creative writing courses (e.g., Forms of Fiction, Memoir, Short Story Cycle) have intentionally forced me to practice my craft while simultaneously examining the tradition of the genre in which I was working. It's not enough for me to attempt to write a short story cycle; I must also study how writers as diverse as Chaucer, Sherwood Anderson, Louise Erdrich, and Joyce Carol Oates have approached the form. Courses such as Classical Myth, Vintage Verse, Shakespeare, and The World Novel have grounded me in the literature that has survived the ages. As a potential professional writer, I have read these texts as models of how to use literary form to explore a subject originally and profoundly. It's been my goal throughout to understand not only the historical and social contexts that formed these texts but also to examine how a Shakespearean tragedy, or an erotic poem by Sappho, or the dark parables of Kafka speak to the paradoxes of our own age. In such courses as Family Systems in Film and Literature, Holy Books, and Women's Literature, I have prompted myself to examine literature through the lenses of psychology, theology, and feminist theory.

Mastery of Methodology

While I hope to write stories and novels, I have attempted in my competence to establish a foundation in many different genres. I care deeply about the process and moral purpose of fiction, but I want my language to be as distilled and resonant as a poem, and I want my narratives to have the veracity and integrity of journalism. While my creative writing courses have been concentrated in fiction (e.g., Sudden Fiction, Forms of Fiction, Short Story Cycle, and an independent study in South American Magical Realism), I have also worked methodically, both in classes and special workshops, on poetry. I have worked for two years, both officially and unofficially, on *The Raven Review*, and have taken additional courses in Writing as Performance and Scriptwriting, which have allowed me to see my stories as performable texts. I have honed my critical writing skills in various literature courses, but at the heart of any creative writing degree is the workshop method. All my creative writing classes revolve around this process. The workshop method gives me what I cannot get by working alone as a writer: it provides a living, critical laboratory for my work. Submitting a story to my peers for discussion offers me an immediate community of (hopefully) generous and honest readers who will help me understand what may have been merely half-conscious and/or ill-formed impulses in the first draft. The workshop forces me to become not just an intuitive writer but an intentional one, not just a spontaneous "gusher" but a disciplined craftsperson and (with any luck) an artist. As a member of a workshop, I also hone my practical critical skills, examining not finished masterpieces but works-in-progress. I learn not only from my own mistakes but also from the successes and mistakes of others, and in the process I begin to develop my own aesthetic. My own body of work, such as it is, is immeasurably stronger because of this ongoing community. And the work and the criticism of my mentors and the students from these classes will inform my future work. They are, as Prescott College President Dan Garvey stated in his inauguration speech, my "significant others." They are the voices in my head.

Interconnections

You must, as a writer, not just understand literature but also understand the world. In order to write with authority and wisdom, you must be insatiably curious. I have embraced my liberal arts education as a way of knowing the world. In order to write about my characters, I must understand them psychologically, socially, ecologically, spiritually, and physically. My memoir of my father's life is not just an autobiographical story; it is informed by my understanding of family systems theory, by my ethnographic field studies, and by my marine biology course set in Kino Bay, Mexico (near where my father was born). My poems are meditations on the mating habits of sea grunion, the spiritual complexities of St. Paul, and the sheer sense of wonder I experienced kayaking around The Sea of Cortez with professor Dave Craig. My news stories for *The Raven Review* forced me to educate myself on local ranching politics, grazing rights, and the economic oppression of Native Americans in Yavapai County. One of the rewards of being a writer is that I don't always have to be myself; I get to, at least imaginatively, be a field biologist, a lawyer, a psychologist, a yoga master, a woman. While my competence has been Creative Writing and Literature, everything I've done as a student here continues and will continue, I hope, to feed into my life's work.

Application of Learning

Pulitzer-Prize winning historian David McCullough said in a recent interview, "The great thing about the arts is that they are applied. You can only learn them by doing them." Writing, like other arts, is by its very nature experiential. All of my courses have allowed me the privilege of seeing myself as an artist. I haven't been just writing stories, poems, essays, articles, and scripts as exercises. The stakes have always been high; everything I've written has been for keeps. Robert Frost once said, "I never write exercises. Sometimes I write poems that fail, and then I call them exercises." That is the way I have approached my competence. As I begin my senior project, I already have a large body of work, "a carcass for my imagination to feed on," as Philip Roth says. I've written, revised, and polished my work. I've sent it out to editors of magazines and journals. I've received thirty-two rejections, four of them with seriously encouraging notes on them, and one letter that apologized for not accepting my sonnet. I have not "succeeded" yet by public standards, but I've entered the arena, and I've received enough encouragement—from mentors, peers, and strangers—that I now believe I have enough talent to be a working writer. Through such courses as Newspaper Journalism Practicum, Literary Journal Practicum, and Writers in the Community, and a teaching assistantship for Writing Workshop, I've also been given the opportunity to work as a semi-professional in my field. My senior project is a collection of stories—expanded from work begun in Short Story Cycle. My experience as an editor, a teaching assistant, a writer in many workshop classes, and a student of literature, particularly fiction, has prepared me to put together what I hope will be my first published book. (If not, I can always call it an exercise.)

Personalization of Learning

In *The Art of Fiction*, John Gardner argues that the process of literature is inevitably moral: "Unexpected connections begin to surface; hidden causes become plain; life becomes, however briefly and unstably, organized; the universe reveals itself, if only for the moment, as inexorably moral; the outcome of the various characters' actions is at last manifest; and we see the responsibility of free will." For me, writing is an intensely personal and spiritual expression of who I am. Even when I'm writing from the perspective of an eighty-year-old Argentinean grandmother, I'm writing autobiographically. I cannot escape my obsessions. Writing poetry, fiction, articles, and plays allows me to investigate the world in minute and visceral ways. And this process forces me to test my own assumptions, to interrogate my own and my culture's psyche, and to articulate to myself an authentic vision of the world, however tenuous that may be. It makes me examine myself, certainly, but the process is not, in the end, an indulgent one. For me, all art, especially fiction writing (because it asks the writer to explore the inner lives of different people), is a constant lesson in compassion. When asked why he prayed, theologian and writer C. S. Lewis responded, "Not because I think it changes the world or because I think God listens, but because it makes me a better person." I write—and I study writing and literature—for the same reason.

An Advisor's Confession

The advising process at Prescott College is highly personalized. Both students and faculty advisors devote a huge amount of time and energy each year to shape each student's Degree Plan and Senior Project Application. It's a challenging advising system but ultimately worth it because it requires us to put into practice our philosophy of student-centered, alternative, experiential education.

Despite my extensive work with advising over the past eleven years, I find myself remembering my own misjudgments, failures, lack of attention, and lack of humility as an advisor. I remember the students who changed advisors, the advisees who withdrew or transferred to different universities, the students who simply disappeared. I remember the students who cried in my office while I dumbly looked on—the appropriate words of consolation coming to me hours later when they were useless. I remember the students who needed a gentler, more compassionate guide than me, the students I should have pushed harder, the students I made excuses for, the students for whom I should have been a more persistent advocate. I remember the exhaustion of Degree Plan deadlines and the anger I felt reading another draft of a Senior Project Application when my comments and scrupulous text editing from the previous draft had been virtually ignored.

I also remember working, laughing, and arguing with my colleagues as we wrote program advising documents, clarified criteria for quantitative and qualitative standards, compiled advising checklists, and discussed the nuanced semantics of "competence," "breadth," and "liberal arts." I remember laboring with advisees over their independent study contracts, Degree Plans, and Senior Project Applications. I remember my first faculty retreat, sharing a yurt with two senior faculty members, and being awakened before dawn to their heated discussion of the politics of our advising process.

Finally, I remember moments of advising clarity and even bliss: field trips, conferences at a bagel shop or on the lawn of the Prescott College Chapel. I remember laughing with students until I couldn't breathe, tears streaming down my cheeks. I remember the great joy of working with advisees on the fifth or eight or tenth incarnation of a Degree Plan, and suddenly seeing them "get it," the light bulb brightening over their heads, and them saying, "Yeah, now I understand what I want to do with my life." I remember the student who cursed me when I demanded a major rewrite of her competence description and then bought me dinner after that final draft was completed, confessing that she finally understood how the process *had* clarified what she'd been striving to do for the past five years. I remember the three students who told me they stayed in school because of my words of encouragement. I remember being moved to tears at every graduation ceremony I've attended. I remember the student who cried during an advising session because his fiancée had just decided to break their engagement. Sitting silently with him, as a witness to his grief, it dawned on me that *this* was what advising was really about. I remember the letters, e-mails, calls, and visits from former advisees who have gone off to live their complicated, fascinating lives—flourishing in graduate school, climbing mountains, joining the Peace Corps, establishing ashrams, writing stories and poems, making films, marrying, having children, starting businesses— all with a philosophical good cheer that swells my heart and makes me grateful to have been part of *their* journeys.

Being a Prescott College faculty advisor is, ultimately, a noble endeavor, a wonderful privilege, even if it is also sometimes difficult and draining. Like parenting, it is a chaotic, spirit-testing adventure, and I often don't feel equal to the task. As with my own children, more often than not I believe that my students and advisees are the real mentors, that it is I who have learned the most, that it is I who have been profoundly transformed.

PART II
EXPERIENTIAL EDUCATION IN PRACTICE

SUSAN HERICKS, PH.D.

What happens when an instructor does not know everything or, worse, makes a mistake? Susan Hericks offers just such a moment, reflecting on the tension that often underlies experiential learning and examining her dual role as a teacher and a learner.

"This shared experience, of student and instructor, adds a crucial learning connection in experiential education," she says. "I wanted to share my developing thoughts about mentoring students non-hierarchically, with honesty, vulnerability, and respect—that is, to write about being real and even fallible with students. And I wanted to think about the value of 'failure' as an aspect of intellectual and spiritual growth for teachers and students alike."

From 2001 to 2003, Susan Hericks was visiting instructor and sabbatical replacement in Religious Studies at Prescott College. She has taught courses in Religion, Philosophy, Ethics, and Dreamwork. Her work with high-risk youth has included planning and carrying out extra-curricular educational programs on topics such as nonviolent communication, drug abuse, sexuality, job preparation, and bullying.

I WISH I WERE DEAD: THE FREEDOM OF FAILURE

ools rush in where angels fear to tread. I have found myself frequently chuckling this maxim to myself during my time at Prescott College (PC). As a new teacher at the college, for better or worse, it sometimes described my *modus operandi* in general. This philosophy was in full flower on the day, at the end of my first year at PC, I asked my colleague Grace Burford to take me to Watpromkunarom (a Thai Buddhist Monastery in the Phoenix area) in order to prepare a future class field trip that I would have to take without her.

Experiential educators agree that we should be willing to experience and to model any task we ask of our students. Ideally, we do this before them and know as much about this task as possible. Perhaps, when we have done something many times before they do—whether it is building a climbing anchor or visiting an inner city school—we forget that not only excitement, but also tension and anxiety can accompany an encounter with the new. Deep down, most of us would agree with TV icon Marge Simpson's assertion, "I fear the unfamiliar." This trip, taken with all the eagerness and enthusiasm of an engaged student, was, for me, a lesson in this state of stress. More than that, it was a lesson in the power that humor and forgiveness have to ease the suffering that often comes with learning.

It is a scorching, spring, Arizona day as we travel to Watprom for the observance of Visakhapuja, the traditional anniversary of the birth, enlightenment, and death of the Buddha. I am in full-on student mode and grateful for Grace's ongoing commentary and instruction. Whereas I am a wide-eyed innocent, Grace is a total pro, both a Buddhist scholar and practitioner. Not only has she visited this temple many times, she has visited Thailand and even speaks some Thai. She is able to greet familiar Sangha members in their language and to chat with the monk who steps forward to host us through the day. She has another advantage that the uninitiated might not immediately appreciate: she is about five feet tall. This matters. At a Thai monastery, which is of the more conservative Theravada branch of Buddhism, a layperson must never be higher than a monk. Sometimes this requirement is fulfilled by the layperson sitting while the monk stands. Throughout the ceremonies and prayers, the Sangha members sit on the floor while the monks sit on a dais; at such times, approaching the monks requires crouching or, more often, walking on the knees.

What do I do, then, when I am taller (much taller and, well, plain big) than a monk and standing next to him? A taller layperson, in this case me, theoretically solves this problem by standing at a distance from the monk. It does not really make me shorter, but it's a matter of perspective. Thanks to the warning of my companion and the graciousness of our host, who occasionally approaches to inform this blond amazon what will be happening next, for most of the day I manage to stay below the monks by shuffling on my knees and standing at a distance.

One disadvantage that Grace and I share in this place is that we are both women. Grace prepared me in advance of the trip, reminding me to cover even my lustful bare toes despite the heat, reminding me women must never touch the monks or be touched by them. Not only that, but if one of the monks wants to give me something, he must put it down or hand it to a layman to hand to me, lest we even touch the same object at the same time. Grace told me that, in the most conservative areas of Thailand, the monks will not even pet a dog before checking the sex.

Transmitting cultural rules to students, as Grace did for me, is one of the burdens of venturing into unfamiliar cultural territory as we try to educate experientially. Especially when there are many differences between the way we ordinarily act in American culture and the way respect requires us to act in another environment, the fear factor for both instructor and students can be high. "What happens if I do something wrong?" the student wonders. The instructor, on the other hand, wonders, "What happens when a mistake is made?" Usually, when we offend it is without even knowing. In the worst case, some students may not listen to instructions or, having listened, disregard the behavioral norms of their hosts.

In a way, the desire not to conform makes sense, which can make the instructor who is asking for conformity (as a sign of respect) all the more uncomfortable. In some cases, we simply cannot see the purpose of certain behavior. In other cases, as one example, the sometimes blatantly sexist practices that we and our students see (or think we see) when observing religious/cultural practices are hard to observe without flinching. Because one aspect of learning about religion is to expand our own ethical norms and consider them in a broader context, it can be extremely challenging to respect what seem to be unethical traditions that perpetuate inequity. A visitor to Watprom witnesses many women serving and a few men receiving. Despite their hard work and piety, women are second-class, culturally, and are obstacles for the monks, spiritually. During meals, which the women of the Sangha prepare and serve, the monks eat first.

Students can be prepared in advance to notice such behavior without overt judgement in the moment and encouraged to deal later, in the van or the classroom, with the cognitive dissonance of witnessing such practices. Much of what we do on field trips is to notice, notice, and notice again—always in wonder, not in judgment. If we can grow toward understanding that learning about a religion is distinct from practicing it, and that religion is inseparable from culture, we can begin to encounter unfamiliar cultures with respect and see our own ideas and practices in comparatively bold relief. When I find myself asking questions such as "Why should I crouch down? Why should I agree to be treated as inferior, impure, lustful? Why should I swelter in shame while the monks each have a beautiful, brown, and completely bare shoulder exposed?!" I begin to notice my own version of "right." I also notice the paternalism that is part and parcel of that outrage—the idea that, in my privilege, I know what is best for others. The discomfort of the new can be due, at least in part, to the novel awareness of our privileges in the presence of those who lack them or who understand privilege in another way altogether. Taken from the latter perspective, in unusual settings we may find that it is we who lack the privileges we are used to, such as the advantage of speaking the common language or having the race of the majority of people present. And we may not like it.

Such discomfort is a teacher in its own right. It reminds us that our perspective is partial, and that to include other perspectives in the effort to learn we will, indeed, suffer the pangs of tension and the letting go of dearly held views.

As I navigate the ceremonies of the day at Watprom, I wonder what leads people to practice in this way. What do these actions have to do with the life of the Buddha and what he experienced? This is not a new question—substitute "Jesus" for "Buddha" and it is a question that, in combination with many other events and ideas, led me to stop attending Christian churches. Is there a way to practice *religion* without perpetuating the oppressive tendencies of *culture*? Are we attempting to make this split when we talk so much about *spirituality* because we are tired of the hypocrisy of *religion*? The hope that we can have a spirituality purified of cultural taint and of the romanticism with which we Americans regard the traditions of Asia cannot stand up to the challenge of experiential learning. To see Thai Buddhists practicing in America is to find something very different than what we learn when we read *What the Buddha Taught*. We encounter a living practice and living people with all the faults and foibles and marvelous particularities that we ourselves embody. We find humans alight with joy or weighed down with bitterness or preoccupied with being correct. We find our own personal and cultural flaws mirrored and magnified by what we hoped would offer a pristine alternative to the contemptuous familiar.

Still, the failure to comply with the different is another unexpected teacher.

At the end of the day I am standing outside the temple, alone, overdressed and baking, pausing to take in the scents of jasmine and basil, roses and orange trees. After the lunch break we finished the day with more prayers and then circumambulation of the temple, following the chanting monks over the radiating pavement carrying incense and candles that Grace and I helped the women tie to flowers. I am glad that the ceremonies are over. I think that Grace will emerge from the temple and we will go, finding a place to change into shorts before heading north to our cooler mountains in Prescott. She doesn't come. I reenter the temple, where Grace stands with the monk who has hosted us all day long. "They want us to sign the guest book," she tells me and, in a flash, with my guard down, I step directly over to the monk; I reach for the guest book he holds in one hand and the pen he holds in the other, touching his fingers. It is one of those endless moments of shame. I feel suspended in my embarrassment. I feel Grace standing behind me, a burning righteous spotlight, sorry that she ever brought me. I am towering over the monk. I am enormous. I grip the guest book, internally shouting to him, "Let go! Let go!" He doesn't.

Amazingly, cool as a cucumber, the monk graciously asks if I would like to sit. "Yes!" I desperately accept. He calmly puts the book down in front of me, and the crisis passes, but not my sense of complete stupidity. With my internal critic already beginning to recount my failure, I only vaguely remember signing the book, telling the monk that I would like to bring students to visit, asking his name and thanking him over and over. And over. Without Grace's instruction, I would never even have known, from his response, that I had blundered, and blundered big.

As I step out of the Temple, the memory of a recent radio interview with author Barbara Kingsolver visits me. In it, she speaks of traveling in Japan, where, as a tall, awkward white woman always doing the wrong thing, she learned and frequently used an apology that literally means "I wish I were dead." As evidence that I am not the only one, I tell Grace about this, about how I wish I had known such a phrase in the moments just past. As we flee to the car I cannot help laughing; it is that or cry.

Despite her presence during the whole horrible scene, I begin to remorsefully recount the travesty that just took place, detail by detail, including the mental and emotional uproar that was not visible. I am trying to apologize, trying to reassure her I am not a total idiot and, fortunately for me, Grace lives up to her name. She is able to laugh with me, not at me, and her levity lets me realize that if the monk can forgive me, I suppose I can forgive myself.

A year later, after telling this story many times to students, friends, and colleagues, I am struck more and more with the appropriateness of the apology "I wish I were dead" and, along with it, the benefits of that uncomfortable feeling of wanting to disappear. No doubt this is a strange assertion, so allow me to explain: The sentiment of wanting to die (metaphorically) is a sign that directs us away from our petulant, unruly egos so that learning can happen and respect can prevail. It says something close to the Buddhist idea of no-self. To die to the false concept of self is to wake up to life as it is, passing and changing continually. It is to be less affected by the stress of such change—the same stress that we face when learning something new. We experience suffering when we hold tightly to our ideas about ourselves and what we believe is true. To make "I wish I were dead" less of a self-destructive apology and more of a learning strategy would be to express it as, "I am willing to change," or "I am willing to experience this moment fully, without judgment." The point here is that when "I" fail, I am challenged to let go of all that "I" am and to become open to other possibilities. Such an effort, even imperfectly realized, can free me and make me aware of choices that I didn't know existed. Later, I will process and interpret; for if I process and interpret from the beginning, I don't have good information to consider.

By letting ourselves be "dead," old ideas give way to new ones; it is an experience that is too often a painful loss and, therefore, we avoid it. Yet, if we sincerely want to learn, we will have to let go of the "I" who already knows it all. This metaphor is not relevant only in Buddhist thought, but Christians have a related concept of "dying to sin" on a daily basis and being reborn constantly. "In life we are in death," the Christian liturgy states, recognizing the change that we constantly experience both in literal death and in the everyday cycles of our lives. While most religious traditions have common ideas of surrendering the self to the divine, this idea of letting go is not only relevant to experiential education in religion but in other areas as well. A beginning climber, for instance, might be thinking, "If I fall I will get hurt." Falling on a climbing rope requires repeated "failure" in order to learn that what was previously believed is not the only option. "If I fall I might get hurt, but most of the time I won't, and, in fact, I can learn to fall skillfully so that I won't get hurt." Letting go of rightness can reduce fear and insecurity, allowing room for other experiences.

The value of my experience has turned out to be different than what I anticipated, both for my students and myself. I thought that I would learn how to plan effective future trips to Watprom, but more than making a visit with students possible, the experience has become a story that I tell my students and that they seem to find as funny as I do. My World Religions class began gleefully referring to this story as the time I "molested" the monk. The story of my own experience of failure and embarrassment builds a bridge of empathy between us. It lets my students know that I, too, am flawed. If I can laugh at myself and invite them to laugh too, their fear of failure and judgment may be softened. So comforted, they may be willing to try things they would not have attempted before. If we can begin to accept these failures, these small surrenders, we may even find joy and connection in them, and we will be able to move on, even in the fear that remains. In responding to this story, my students have also practiced compassion by forgiving me; they have seen me as real and accepted me as a fellow learner who is sometimes, but not always, ahead. With such empathy and compassion around, we can indeed rush in where angels fear to tread, and we will find ourselves enriched by whatever experience we have.

ALISON HOLMES

The relationship that needs to exist between student and teacher permeates "Experiencing the Integrative Work of the Liberal Arts." In this essay, Alison Holmes demonstrates the necessary work of full response to wholes rather than the more common building of totalities through reaction. And through the joining of experience and expression, she reveals the nature of the human experiment from the inside out.

"It is difficult to write specifically about an intuitive moment of consciousness," Holmes says. "In this piece, there is a blending of perspectives, ranging from specific steps and exercises to the philosophical justifications for them."

Born and raised in China, Alison Holmes was educated in China and at Oxford University. An educator for over forty years, Holmes has been on the faculty at Prescott College since 1988.

EXPERIENCING THE INTEGRATIVE WORK
OF THE LIBERAL ARTS

"And what you thought you came for
Is only a shell, a husk of meaning
From which the purpose breaks only when it is fulfilled
If at all"

            -T.S. Eliot (from "Little Gidding")

In the moment before the curtain goes up, before I meet the cast who will be attending the weekend Liberal Arts Seminar, I mentally fill the room. It is five o'clock on a cold, winter evening as I stand in the Sam Hill building, a large, old warehouse with warm brick walls, wooden pillars and rafters, a wood floor, and windows that are covered this evening by sliding doors held together with great iron bars. There is a table with flowers, bowls of organic fruits, homemade pizza and brownies; coffee urns are perking. Soon, in the circle of empty chairs by the window, I will see a few young graduates from the University of Arizona seeking teacher certification, a Navajo medicine man, a retired policeman, a chartered accountant, an organic farmer, a Mormon mother of nine, a wildlife preservationist from Alaska, a young Pennsylvania Dutch couple, and a casino worker who wants to counsel recovering alcoholics like himself. In all, there will be twenty to twenty-five students, depending on who has missed a plane, experienced washed out roads, or had a medical emergency.

This diverse group is attending a mandatory seminar to fulfill a residency requirement for the Adult Degree Program (ADP), essentially a distance-learning program offered by the college. As members of this community-based program, the students come from all over the country, some from beyond this country—from Japan, Switzerland, and Ecuador. It is not easy to travel to Prescott, Arizona, to find lodging, to pull one's self away from family, job, and all that makes for the complications and joys of daily living. It is a situation calculated to create a mixture of unease, resentment, resignation and, perhaps, a little excitement.

So what does Prescott College want this experience to be? What is the point of this seminar? The aim is easy to define: it is to develop critical thinking and to work with its values of integration in both individuals and the group as a whole. It's about observing and understanding the different orientations used in fulfilling and sustainable lives. It's about enhancing perspective and seeing the liberal arts in a new light.

There is an understandable fuzziness, in general, about what the liberal arts are and what their value is. On the one hand we have the Noah's Ark approach (take two of these arbitrary subjects, two of those, and hope that when the ark lands after the flood they will go forth and multiply somehow). On the other hand, we hear that the business world seeks those who are not vocationally trained but who have, thanks to their liberal arts degree, the ability to range widely and dig deeply. Is there perhaps a third approach? Could we say that the dictum, "Know thyself," has always been the key to all knowledge and fulfillment? Has that been the motivation behind all true education? And what does it mean? Are we required to move beyond content and skills to direct experience, experience first as an inner dynamic and then as an outer application? Experience has to be a whole, integrating first the individual and then, in the fullest way possible, integrating us to the whole of which we are a part.

A colleague of mine once said, "Literature, the love of a good woman, and a liberal arts education transformed my life!" How is one to orchestrate such a transformation, such an integration (in such a diverse group) in so short a time? The answer is, of course, that it is not possible. But perhaps there can be a structure that encourages a beginning to such a movement.

Structure is implicit in the whole mission of Prescott College. We emphasize the value of the self-directed journey as opposed to the handing down of accumulated knowledge and technique. We have years of experience that demonstrate that this journey leads not only to successful achievement of degrees but also to transformation in the students. In the Adult Degree Program, we have identified five formal vehicles to aid the student in self-direction: 1. orientation, 2. a course in critical issues and application, 3. individually chosen course work accomplished within the mentor system, 4. a liberal arts seminar, 5. a synthesizing essay in each student's graduation portfolio. Each element builds upon the others in a continuum that provides opportunity for thought and the discovery of unfolding meaning in the personal, the educational, and the communal arenas.

This continuum is echoed in miniature in the weekend seminar's structure. It begins with the individual response, continues with discussion in small groups, moves on to a group focus of analysis and synthesis, and culminates in the development of individual projects that affect the community at large. The design of the seminar is intentionally simple so that there is room for individual discovery. There is no script, no checklist of activities; a lurch from focus to focus would only encourage separation and fragmentation. Each group is always an experiment. Each group is always weighted differently in terms of ability to be consciously present, thoughtfully alive to the encounters with theme, with text, and with the other participants. In fact, the course description echoes this goal: "This course will be an examination of the concepts of . . . the liberal arts through literature, politics, science, psychology, and personal integration. It is an experiment, an experience, and an expression of creative critical thinking."

As this seminar is the only course which students do not design themselves, it is easy to see old patterns kick in: "What does this teacher want me to say?" "What am I supposed to write here?" People get ill, fail to find a baby sitter, forget deadlines, and are generally overwhelmed.

Fear lurks just beneath the surface, no matter how reassuring the cover letter students receive with their pre-seminar assignments is. They have been asked to write response papers on the readings and also to do three or four other exercises such as responding to prompts like, "We are told that a given map is not the territory. Take yourself for a walk. Make a map of the area and then note down all you could not include in this map." It is abundantly clear to me that it is impossible for anyone to use her mind creatively if she is struggling with anxiety. So, I spend time on the phone speaking to the difference between a mandatory course and one done under compulsion. The framework may have been supplied, but all that is required from the student is an open mind, a willingness to be curious and to wonder. It is necessary to reiterate that this is an experiential course and that much of the learning will be done together at the weekend. Once students hear this, once they are reassured that the pre-seminar assignments are there just to allow their minds to wander around a theme, to discover their own individual approach to the topic, I can hear them relax. Encouraged to accept and acknowledge where they stand, they often use this moment of contact to speak of their situation at home or at work. This phone call not only releases a compulsive straining after what the students had perceived to be required, but it encourages a relaxed focus on the material and starts to create the field of relationship for the weekend. I may speak to a student as many as ten times via telephone or e-mail, clarifying and reassuring.

It is essential to spend time working through the papers submitted by each student ten days before the seminar, to make rough psychological profiles of each student, to assess who struggles with concepts, who is dissociated and reactive, who is mentally acute and receptive. Too often, the effects of old methods of teaching are evident once again on their writing. Students are fearful of encountering the new; they have either become passive, overwhelmed by information, or they have learned to handle the onslaught by rebellion or dissociation. Use of Jung's typology (sensing, feeling, thinking, and intuiting) serves as an anchor for this informal analysis of each student and provides a guide as to what the predominant tone of the seminar will be. As the aim of the seminar is to develop all four functions in an integrated movement, this typology works well. Without the integration of the emotional and the mental, a student cannot make a full response to the contact of both material and circumstance, cannot be creatively present with critical inquiry and discerning attitudes.

So in students come, tired from long drives, plane flights, concerned about their nights' lodging, about how their partners will occupy themselves over the weekend, and about whom they themselves are going to encounter in the next three days. It is important that I have a sense of who each one is—their preoccupations of the moment, their fears, their senses of humor—so I am able to greet them as individuals already known and valued. This creates an easy and reassuring tone that is maintained in the opening circle. I outline the structure of the weekend and provide stories and examples of final projects completed by other students. These projects can range from writing one hundred poems in celebration of Native American culture to getting a whole school involved in a lunch program for the homeless, from creating an explanatory book for a five-year-old with Mitochondrial Disease to working with prisoners in Habitat for Humanity. This variety demonstrates that students really can work as individuals and with what moves them. Once the overview is sketched out for them, the students are ready to present themselves to their colleagues.

Students are asked to share the usual details (name, hometown, area of academic study), but they have also been asked to prepare an introduction that includes a personal story relevant to the seminar's theme. For example, if the seminar is "Freedom and the Liberal Artist," students are asked to tell us of a time when they felt intensely free. If the seminar is "Signals and Symbols," students speak of the symbol that has had most power in their lives, not merely of what it is supposed to represent but what has made it meaningful to them, how it has opened them up to consistently increased understanding.

The introductions, these stories, allow the speaker and the listeners to engage at a deeper level, providing the opportunity for humor, for depth, for the qualities of the student to come forward. Hearing others reflect on their individual experiences helps the more timid ones realize they can say more than, "When I graduated from high school and moved into my first apartment…." They abandon their prepared stories for something more essential. This courage resonates deeply and gives everyone a vivid sense of each other. Students also begin to realize that there are a variety of ways to look at a theme, as they see relationships between physical, emotional, and mental approaches to the same topic.

The formal structure within which students see that all these approaches contribute to a whole (or at least to a more complete picture) is outlined briefly in the functions of our threefold brain. This is done very lightly and easily. If we are going to work on critical thinking, it is important that we actually have an idea of what the biology of thought is. A simple sketch done on the board of the triune brain is both referred and added to throughout the weekend. Though we often function physically and psychologically at the very basic level of fight or flight (Shall I eat it? Will it eat me?), we are capable of functioning at a higher level than this. We trace the movement from the reptilian through the limbic to the neo-cortex, each area independent yet interdependent, each area capable of bringing information to the thinking process, yet all required if the reaction is to move through relationship into a full response. This integration of all three, this progressive enfoldment into larger contexts, allows us to move into the world of critical thinking. Once higher order thinking skills are theoretically understood by all, it is time to experience them. Our goal is to move beyond reaction to the theme of the seminar, beyond an exchange of opinions, valuable as that is, to wrestling with ideas.

The group is divided into small groups of four or five students each. They are asked to work together, to brainstorm, to discover a vocabulary that can be shared over the weekend, a doorway into the theme that can be accepted by all. On butcher paper, with colored markers, they "mind map," argue, and laugh. The groups are small enough to ensure that each person contributes, be it with graphics, anecdotes, or analytic thought Each group approaches the task differently, but each group is looking for what lies behind their immediate impressions. The discovery of these underlying patterns leads to the discovery of deeper meaning, especially when all the different representations of their thoughts are shared with the larger group. Sometimes the presentation is linear, bullet point by bullet point, sometimes a circular or spiral awareness of flow and interdependence, sometimes an organic cosmology or a beautiful tree with roots firmly tucked in soil, strong trunk, and fruit on branches. The opportunity to see this variety, with its differences and commonalities, is the beginning of shared experience and thought. They have begun to have a sense of the group as a whole and have sparked enough ideas to send them off into the night, tired but stimulated.

Saturday morning, we gather again in the Sam Hill building, a space that offers itself so easily to all of the activities of the weekend. There is room for breakout discussion groups, room for the breakfast table, room for stretching exercises, all in the shelter of this great, sunlit room. Sunshine pours through the south-facing windows, throwing dappled shadows on the wooden floor. Often someone will step forward to offer us a way to greet the day. It may be basic yoga poses. It may be an awareness of our breath. A coach may get us all doing jumping jacks, or we may become howling Viking warriors. It doesn't always happen, but when it does it leads to an easy bonding of the group, to laughter and an awareness of a variety of styles of being at home in the body. It allows for a different contribution to the group dynamic, and it also shakes up those who are not morning people.

Awake, we sit together, reviewing the thoughts and definitions of the night before and revisiting the structure of thought itself. It is key to facilitate the students' organization of what they have experienced into a coherent pattern. If the allegory of Plato's cave has been one of their readings, it can easily be woven in to strengthen that pattern. Are there similar levels seen in that allegory? Are we chained, looking at the shadows on the wall? Do we stop by the fire? Do we go out of the cave into the increasing light of day? Do we stop at the instinctive or at the conditioned fixation, or do we move beyond emotion to feeling and on to creative and critical thinking? The whole loop of consciousness—from focus to awareness, through perspective and recognition, to inspiration— is reemphasized. The students learn to work from a place of inner-discovery first and then to its application in their interactions with others. The parallels they immediately draw from their lives are striking. Teaching into the development of consciousness of consciousness, of observing the mind at work, according to personal and group wholeness, allows them to react, respond, question, evaluate and synthesize, consciously. This is critical thinking in action.

In the pre-seminar assignment, the students read five or six articles from a variety of viewpoints. The texts, ranging from Vandana Shiva and Martin Luther King to Viktor Frankl and the Dalai Lama, speak strongly and clearly of discovering wholeness from a place of personal clarity which then has had outer ramifications. That's what we are striving for, the learning that comes from approaching a topic from a point of creative tension, between what we know and what there is to know, between what we feel and what we think, what we know and what the others know, always reaching, always discovering.

We may work through all of the readings in small group discussions or deal with only one or two of them. The key questions unique to each seminar (e.g. What is freedom? Has it ever been achieved? What are the limitations imposed on freedom?) are applied to the readings. The students may vacillate between a "bull session" and a real awareness of mediating between their understanding and the material, between saying what they already know and entering a place where they don't know. And in that place of unknowing, the true learner has the awareness to hover, waiting to see what coalesces, what forms out of this synergy between what she has read, thought, and felt, and what the group has to offer. The need to listen for those who speak easily and the need to articulate half-formed thoughts for those who are reticent to speak, may be a real struggle. Many times, an apparently peripheral thought will open up a fruitful avenue of exploration. Other times, it may just be a red herring.

The seminar's core questions provide a framework for discussion, but there is no fixed time frame. Depending on the sophistication of the sub-groups, there may be a flowering of thought that ranges wide and deeply, or there may only be a brisk half hour dispatch of the question. Each day, each session requires, as it develops, a constant flexibility. As facilitator, I monitor the movement of each group. Are there clear lines of thought developing? Is there passionate discourse? Are they floundering? Is everyone on the same page? Is it time to introduce a simple exercise to reveal how easily we judge without context? (For example, one half of the group has objects or pictures presented without a context and the other has the identical ones with a fuller background or descriptive label. When asked to describe the qualities such as, "Is this man to be trusted or admired?" many will leap into projections and assumptions.) Should we continue with a larger group discussion to follow up on the issues raised? De we need to explore what it is we actually need for real discernment? Always, there is recapping, review, and clarification of the ideas that have emerged.

Given the fact that these students have worked on their own throughout the program until now, it is totally appropriate that they should rejoice in this opportunity to be with each other, exchanging stories, making suggestions, and sharing their frustrations and challenges—personal, academic and societal. Critical thinking is not just intellection, the mind fidgeting at a topic. The whole person, heart and soul, history and dreams, is present. When that whole person is acknowledged, an integrated response to each other is possible. Whether it is struggles with addiction to prescription drugs or difficulties in finding a mentor, students start becoming supportive of each other.

On Saturday afternoon we often bump up against that moment that comes two-thirds of the way through a workshop when tempers fray, opinions are held on to just for the sake of holding on to them, and no one wants to hear the seminar theme word ever again. I am reminded of the phrase in Plato's Cave, of the prisoners being "reluctantly dragged." It is not me who is doing the dragging, but it is the struggle to shift from unconscious to conscious, the need to leave the comfort zone of past conditioning to move into the responsibility of mediation that can drain energy.

When five o'clock comes, the students are free to go and enjoy the area's great hiking or Whisky Row (Prescott's row of pubs and restaurants). Many of them, however, just go back to their hotels to sleep, exhausted after exercising their minds in a new and continuous way.

I go home and write a handout for the next day, clarifying our thinking process. Even if there are three successive seminars on the same topic, my Saturday evening thoughts are always different. Sometimes the last group gets all three handouts so that they can see how very different the journey has been for others working on the same theme.

The last morning usually opens with a wonderful exercise that marks a shift. Now that they are rested, the students are ready to reengage with the dynamic process. They are given twenty minutes in which to write a two-part exercise. The first paragraph is a careful, detailed account of an experience with light: natural light, starlight, moonlight, candlelight, firelight, sunlight, etc. The second paragraph shows the effect the scene has on the student. They describe their emotional and mental states briefly and then show how the light affects them. They bring their inner and outer worlds together so that they see how the physical light enlightens them, how they are being illuminated, what they feel at having been transformed. In groups, they each share what it felt like to have "the light go on," what the lingering effects of the experience have been, and what new understandings have been gained.

As the morning light streams through the window onto our circle, the organic farmer speaks of a rainbow over his cornfields, the Navajo medicine man of the firelight of the peyote ceremony, and the wildlife preservationist of Northern Lights dancing in Alaska. We hear of swimming in phosphorescent oceans, of candlelit rooms, chess games by moonlight, sunrise after an ice storm. Sometimes we just get narrative, sometimes catharsis, sometimes powerful clarity on personal integration. But always, this experience of synthesizing inner and outer reveals a beauty and a truth that students own and that they can communicate to others. The integration of physical, emotional, mental, the reptilian, the limbic and the neo-cortex leads to the place where the intuition comes into glorious play. It's a gift, consciously made, to the group.

The final discussion is carried out as a group ensemble. The students demonstrate that they know each other's minds, can work with each other and create a structure of thought in search of meaning. It is a pleasure to see the depth, ease, and coherence that has developed amongst them during these few days. The two nights and the two-hour lunch break on Saturday have provided time for raising questions at a deeper level, for reflection, for absorption, for integration. Many of the recurring themes, difficulties, and running jokes reemerge in an enhanced context. It is an easy step now for the students to think about their final projects, a synthesis of their ongoing discoveries.

The final project asks students to choose something they really want to explore, linking heart and mind for the benefit of others. This leads to much talk in small groups. Should it be publishing articles on organic farming? Making a video on alternative energy? Turning a restaurant over to the needy for Christmas? Painting a mural for a women's shelter? They help each other refine ideas, catch fire from suggestions and triumphantly write in objectives and activities on their contracts.

Students are also asked, in their small groups, to formulate a definition of the liberal arts to demonstrate a clear understanding of what has been accomplished over the weekend. The definitions are often both unique and unified, such as the following recent effort: "The liberal artist connects between disciplines, draws from inner and outer experiences, sees from different perspectives, allows exploration and discovery, maintains open-mindedness, [and] examines with critical thinking, synthesizing diverse elements of life with the purpose of transforming everyday life into a creative process."

I delight in hearing the variety of ways students make the liberal arts their own and even more in hearing what they have individually discovered as they speak in the final circle.

The closing circle is the students' opportunity to reflect spontaneously on the weekend and demonstrates the level of assimilation and integration that has taken place. Sometimes the comment is a brief thank you. Sometimes it is a grateful account of a movement towards transformation. There is appreciation of each other and of the learning experience, a heightened sensitivity, a deeper understanding. This appreciation applies particularly to the exchanges that have been made between diverse ethnic groups and cultures; there is gratitude for expanded horizons.

The last thing that remains to be done is to hold individual meetings with each student to sign learning contracts and to wrap up the weekend experience. This is an opportunity I value enormously. While we speak, the other students are able to continue building relationships with each other. Some, of course, are itching for the chance to drive home and pick up their busy lives once again. The seminar is not magic for everyone, but for the right person at the right time, everything lines up perfectly. For these students, this experience of our experiment in critical thinking changes them and they are reluctant to abandon this community of learners, to leave the sun-filled building.

The week after the seminar, evaluations arrive. Often, I discover in these thoughtful critiques that the students truly have experienced much more than the shell, the "husk of meaning," they were expecting. Some students have written of the sense of dread with which they had contemplated the seminar before the weekend. Ruefully, but honestly and without anxiety, they recall their resistance, their fear of not being good enough, their fear of an assumed "touchy, feely" weekend, anxiety at the thought of sitting with total strangers and having to argue together over the merits of varying points of view. And then comes their delight at what the experience had actually been: "The core of this seminar's intent, it seemed to me, was to teach the students to be holistic in our approach to learning. We were discouraged from purely intellectual, linear thinking. We were encouraged to use all aspects of ourselves, such as our emotions and spirituality." The students write of discovering essential commonalties, of exploring individual differences, and of communal contributions.

Such responses do not come from having experienced a bag of tricks, from techniques, however polished. They come from learning that engages with life. It is easy enough to give a list of activities, and these have been included because these activities are part and parcel of the purpose and the goal of the seminar. But what really happens? As the poet Juan Ramon Jimenez writes, "Nothing happens? Or has everything happened / And are we standing now, quietly, in the new life?"

The goal of the seminar is the same as that of the college: self-directed transformative education. The opportunity is offered for all of us (students and faculty) to engage human consciousness as it is meant to be engaged, as a whole. Ideally, the movement of this course is the same for each one of us: quiet and honest preparation, awareness that there is more to discover, peaceful resting in that creative tension, ongoing reflection at each stage, and then delight in the moments where intuition illuminates the whole.

The discovery of our own figure of energy, our own psychological profile, is where we move into knowing ourselves. The subsequent integration and individuation allows for an enhanced perspective that then displays our connectedness with others. It comes from experiencing the transition from a motivation of strictly personal reactivity to that of an integrated, aware intentionality. Instead of reaction, we have the fullest possible response to the contact of as much of the whole as we can experience We stand at the intersection between the quantitative and the qualitative, and at that crossroads we mediate between the inner and the outer. We are required to be present.

There can be no true learning without personal integration. When integration occurs, we can reach out to the greater community to discover together the change that is needed for a sane world. How do we constantly engage in the reflection that keeps our learning alive and discovering? Maybe we really need to be working in small groups, sitting down together and talking. Maybe we need to look at the knowledge handed down to us and see what of it is still relevant. Maybe we need to create and experience an environment for discovery. Too often we are reductive in our concept of the environment, seeing it as trees, mountains, wetlands, all objective things out there, whereas in fact the environment is us, it's the relationships we are capable of, it's everything we contact with our senses, our sensibility, our understanding. It is the liberating art of seeing what is actually there, what the pattern is that lies behind the form. It is tapping in to the essence of thought, moving beyond information, beyond our personal manipulation of knowledge, to the place of meaning and universal wisdom.

Cathedrals no longer bring us together in shared culture. The mall may not offer much for reflection. But, perhaps, gathering in an old brick building gives us a sense of context where we can imagine the future together.

K.L. Cook and Wayne Regina

Interdisciplinary team teaching may sound ideal, allowing students to explore the space between two disciplines under the guidance of an instructor from each field. But once you have sold the course to administration (which is no easy task in itself), how do you approach the intellectual and interpersonal rigor required for effective interdisciplinary team teaching? And how do you reach the synergy that you're certain you, your colleague, and the course are capable of achieving?

In this essay, K.L. (Kenny) Cook and Wayne Regina explore the challenges, risks, and rewards of interdisciplinary team teaching through a course entitled, Family Systems in Film & Literature. *In the end, they found that, despite the hard work and challenges, "The experience enriched both our personal friendship and our professional lives."*

K.L. Cook is a professor of English. He is widely published in literary and scholarly journals, magazines, and newspapers. (For more biographical information, see page 45.)

Wayne Regina, Psy.D. is a systems psychologist and Peace Studies and Human Development professor, specializing in families, organizations, and mediation. His essays have appeared in journals such as Mediation Quarterly *and* Practical Applications in Supervision, *and he is a member of the editorial board for* Journal of Family Dynamics of Addiction. *Prior to joining Prescott College in 1992, he was Associate Professor of Psychology at United States International University.*

Interdisciplinary Team Teaching: *Family Systems in Film & Literature*

Interdisciplinary team teaching is not for the faint of heart. It requires stamina, intellectual and interpersonal rigor, and a willingness to step off the firm footing and comfort of one's own discipline and engage with another professional and students in the realm of a less familiar and more unknown discipline. The unique opportunities and challenges in interdisciplinary team teaching, however, offer both students and teachers the possibility of integrating their learning in intellectually innovative ways.

This essay explores the potential and pitfalls of interdisciplinary team teaching through a course, entitled *Family Systems in Film & Literature*, which we have taught twice at Prescott College. The first half of the essay discusses our experience with interdisciplinary team teaching, including how we developed the course, how we created a vocabulary for understanding each other's ways of seeing the world, how the course pushed us to clarify the manner in which film and literature can be used to animate family systems theory, and how family systems theory can illuminate the creative process in film and literature. We also explore our successes and setbacks during the two times the course was taught and how we modified and adjusted the course content and process to make it more successful in meeting our professional and the students' academic needs and interests.

The second half of the essay describes the practical aspects of interdisciplinary team teaching: institutional support and roadblocks, personal and professional rewards and challenges, and how this kind of course can serve as a model for education that emphasizes interdisciplinary connections rather than disciplinary specialization. We offer suggestions for faculty seeking to emulate this model and for administrators interested in fostering an interdisciplinary curriculum.

While we use our particular class as a case study, our primary intention is to explore the nature of interdisciplinary team teaching. As longtime teachers and administrators at Prescott College, we believe that we bring special insights to this relatively under-explored realm of experiential education.

The Origin and Evolution of *Family Systems in Film & Literature*

We both arrived at Prescott College in the summer of 1992. We came here because of our shared passion for interdisciplinary work as well as our attraction to the college's environmental and social justice mission. Entering with the same cohort group of new faculty, we immediately found a professional and personal kinship, spending many hours discussing our mutual interest in expressions of the human condition through film, literature, and theory.

Over the years, our professional and personal collegiality and friendship blossomed, and we began exploring possible ways to bring our literary, theoretical, and cinematic interests together in an interdisciplinary, team-teaching environment. In essence, *Family Systems in Film & Literature* evolved from our desire, as friends and colleagues, to see our professional worlds through the eyes of the other. We started with a basic line of inquiry: Why do writers and filmmakers seem to be natural family systems theorists, understanding intuitively such family systems concepts as triangulation, chronic anxiety, differentiation, and multi-generational emotional process? How can family systems theory illuminate the serious study of film and literature? Can film and literature be used as a laboratory for studying family systems theory, clarifying and articulating complex concepts that are sometimes difficult to observe inside one's original family?

These questions and others ultimately led to more practical, pedagogical questions. Could a psychologist and writer coexist in the same classroom? Would our excitement about, and respect for, one another and each other's disciplines serve as a model for our students' own interdisciplinary development? How would we go about teaching both disciplines in an intensive, one-month seminar without shortchanging either discipline? And the most important question was this: What special insights lay in the spaces between our disciplines rather than in the disciplines themselves, and how would our students help each other and us discover those insights?

These questions were posed against the backdrop of Prescott College itself. In addition to its interdisciplinary focus and environmental and social justice mission, we were attracted to Prescott College because of its commitment to small, student-centered classes (12-14 students is the maximum class size and the average is just ten) and its dedication to progressive, experiential education. For example, at Prescott College, students do not have "majors" but rather develop "competences," which include coursework, independent studies, internships, and a capstone senior project that must address five central criteria: literacy in the field of study, mastery of methodology, application of learning, personalization of learning, and interconnection of learning. Arguably the most important of these criteria for competence, and certainly for an interdisciplinary course, is interconnection of learning. Unlike larger liberal arts institutions, where team teaching and cross-disciplinary learning and teaching raises significant budgetary and curricular turf battles, Prescott College believes that both students and teachers thrive in an educational environment where they are challenged to clarify underlying assumptions about how to understand the world. In effect, students are asked to train their attention on the ways disciplines intersect with and inform each other, rather than simply acquiring disciplinary knowledge and specialization.

Our course developed slowly over a six-year period. Part of this pace was intentional, as we explored different ideas about interdisciplinary team teaching, and part of this pace was due to circumstance as we both moved into important administrative roles to serve the college and thus minimized our direct teaching obligations.

Once we submitted the course for curricular approval in the spring of 1997, our preparation and planning began in earnest. We decided early on to use a broad-based and flexible model for film and literature, focusing on film clips, short features, full-length features, short stories, plays, and novellas. Due to the condensed nature of a four-week block course, we decided against using full-length novels. Perhaps more importantly, we agreed to target a single theoretical model, that of Bowen Family Systems Theory. Bowen theory has the advantage of being a family systems approach derived from observing natural systems and applying these observations to the family. Among the family systems approaches, Bowen theory is uniquely suited for the minds of our environmental and social justice-based students. In addition, Bowen theory is a comprehensive theoretical system that is intellectually rich, pragmatically sound, and both elegant in its simplicity and complex in its application. It would be well suited to handle the variety of cinematic and literary families that we intended to explore.

Early on, we decided that while we would articulate cinematic and literary elements in films and literature, the central focus of the course would be to help students develop an understanding of family systems theory *through* film and literature. As such, the central goal of the course, as stated in the course syllabus, was "to foster an understanding and application of family systems theory through intellectual and artistic investigation and personal application." In addition, we decided that the intersection of the two disciplines would serve as the leading edge of the course. Again, from the first goal articulated in the syllabus: "This isn't two courses in one. Instead, we envision this course as a true synthesis to help you discover tools and cross-disciplinary ways of seeing, which you can apply to your explorations of family systems theory, literature, film, the creative process, and your own life."

In essence, we wanted to use the theoretical lens of Bowen Family Systems Theory to understand the nature of literary and cinematic expression while simultaneously illuminating the personal world of the family for both the students and the instructors.

Assignments and Projects: Structure vs. Flexibility

Having defined our theoretical perspective for the course and the nature of our interdisciplinary focus, we began searching for appropriate literary and cinematic material. Part of the challenge was the wealth of excellent films and stories available. We sorted through films, books, plays, and short stories to find fictional families that best illustrated the central concepts of Bowen theory. We selected the following films: *Life Lessons, Grand Canyon, What's Eating Gilbert Grape, The Glass Menagerie, Hanna and Her Sisters,* and *Hamlet.* We allowed students to pick several films as well, though their selections reflected cultural influences through the mass media and were less helpful in articulating systemic concepts. In addition, we decided to supplement our classroom time with a local field trip to a movie theatre to view a new release and an outing to a regional theater to attend a play.

We eventually narrowed our reading list and chose two novellas by Jane Smiley, *Ordinary Love and Good Will,* and a Tennessee Williams play, *The Glass Menagerie.* We developed a *Family Systems in Film and Literature* reader as well. This reader contained extensive articles and chapters on Bowen theory by Edwin Friedman, Michael Kerr, Monica McGoldrick, and Randy Gerson. The reader also collected a number of short stories by a variety of authors, including work by John Cheever, James Baldwin, Mona Simpson, Jessica Treadway, and Alice Walker. Finally, we included a number of short stories by two Prescott College writing and literature faculty, K.L. Cook and Melanie Bishop, and planned on a day in which both authors would talk about the transformation of their own family material into fiction.

In developing the reading list, we were careful to provide a balanced gender perspective so that we could examine the theory from the works of both men and women. As a theory that purports universality, we believed it important to explore Bowen Family Systems Theory through a variety of cultural and gender perspectives.

Next, we developed a series of assignments to track student progress, promote interpersonal and intrapersonal development, and encourage creative expression. We designed the class as "writing intensive," a writing-across-the-curriculum designation at Prescott College that imbeds significant analytical writing, revising, and peer review assignments within the content of the course. We chose early on to try and replicate for our students the kind of fruitful dialogue that we experienced while working with each other to develop and implement the course. So, in addition to the formal assignments we asked students to complete, we also asked them to turn in weekly "cover letters"—lengthy epistles in which they summarized what they'd learned and how they'd been studying, synthesizing, and applying family systems theory to literature, film, and their own lives. The cover letters also created a forum for them to carry on a dialogue with us about how the class was going for them—delights, insights, frustrations, questions, suggestions—and how they were meeting the terms of their individual learning contracts. In turn, we wrote them long letters back. The letters became, in some ways, our favorite part of the students' weekly portfolios. They gave us greater insight into their lives and learning styles, personalized their education for us, and provided an effective venue for all of us to communicate, make adjustments, and address complicated issues of either the content or of the class dynamics and structure. Ultimately, it allowed us to articulate and record the learning and teaching process and gave us another way of carrying on a dialogue not only with the students but also with each other. This proved especially useful as we returned to the course for its second and now third incarnations. We have, in essence, a rich and thorough log of our experience.

Personalization of learning, another of the five essential criteria for learning at Prescott College listed above, became a crucial subtext for teaching the course. We reinforced this subtext by having students develop personal genograms, which are factual and emotional family histories that focus on delineating qualitative relationships, themes, patterns, and legacies within a multi-generational context. In creating these genograms, students would come to appreciate the rich systemic context of their personal lives and begin exploring ways to differentiate or emotionally separate themselves from the automatic and reactive processes inherent in their families. This personalization exercise would culminate with students presenting their genograms to the class.

We realized, of course, that to ask students to bare their family histories and stories to the entire class, we would first have to bare *our* family histories and stories. It is this kind of emotionally and intellectually challenging work that helps us, as teachers, stay alive and grow, while creating an appropriate climate for our students. The degree to which students feel safe investigating and sharing their own stories depends upon the degree that we, as instructors, are willing to examine ourselves. In fact, we believe this combination of the theoretical with the personal accomplishes twin goals: students find intellectual value in analyzing fictional families, and they find personal value in applying these theoretical insights to their own extended families. We hoped this shared experience regarding all of our families would be emotionally moving and also help normalize family processes; students would realize that *all* multi-generational families have histories that include trauma, challenges, and resiliency.

In addition to the portfolio packets, cover letters, and multi-generational genograms, we decided on additional assignments, including an application essay, meant to give students the opportunity to apply specific aspects of family systems theory to one or more of the texts or movies that we would study. This multi-draft essay was designed to deepen students' understanding of the theory through application to the "texts" (both literary and cinematic) that we studied.

Lastly, we developed a creative application assignment, designed for small groups to present some aspect of Bowen theory through film and literature that would include an experiential class presentation.

FSFL: First Incarnation

We taught the course for the first time in the Winter Block of 1998. While Wayne's *Family Systems Theory* classes predominantly enrolled human development and psychology students, *Family Systems in Film & Literature* attracted, as we had hoped, students from a wider population, including a number of writing and literature students. Drawing students from differing academic perspectives helped us immediately to highlight a cross-disciplinary approach.

While many students initially blanched at the significant reading and writing in this four-week course, most everyone rose to the occasion, completing all of the assignments. In fact, students quickly embraced the theory as they were fascinated by its richness, complexity, and comprehensiveness. All of the assignments were quite valuable, adding to students' learning and our assessment of their progress.

On the very first day, we read in class Raymond Carver's two-page story, "Popular Mechanics," a tragic tale depicting an argument between a couple who are separating. Their tension escalates as they fight over who will retain custody of their child. In a scene eerily reminiscent of Solomon and the two mothers fighting over possession of the baby, the two parents in the end of the story each grab the baby and literally "rend" the child in two. "In this manner," the omniscient narrator says in the darkly ironic final line, "the issue was decided." While the class began to decipher what had happened in the story and its symbolic meaning, we quickly focused their attention on the family systems concepts of Bowen theory. While the story may resonate as a contemporary parable about the tragic ramifications of parental strife, it also brilliantly and efficiently dramatizes the concepts of emotional triangles and triangulation, the nature of automatic emotional reactivity, anxiety cascades and system runaways. Our goal in this short exercise was to begin to train the students how to apply the theory to the text, and how to use the text to illustrate and humanize the theory.

On this same day, we watched Martin Scorsese's short film, *Life Lessons*, about a famous middle-aged painter (played by Nick Nolte) and his young assistant (played by Roseanna Arquette). The film, in Bowen terms, depicts the artist's attachment to his art and to the girl, with whom he has had an affair, and how both sex and art become anxiety binders for him. We see him generating his own and his assistant's chronic anxiety and then trying to triangulate (even exorcise) that anxiety through his art. We also witness the stark difference between the artist's *basic* differentiation level (that is, his emotional maturity) and his *functional* differentiation level, which deteriorates as the film progresses and he becomes consumed by his own violent jealousy.

This kind of exploration and analysis led to a rapid engagement with the artistic and theoretical material and immediately set the intellectual tone for the course. By the end of the first week, students were working in small groups, explicating the theory for the rest of the class, prompted by assigned topics such as the following:

- What is the concept of the emotional triangle? Using examples from the literature and films we've studied, chart several central and interlocking triangles and compare and contrast the way anxiety moves through the different emotional systems. Specify the anxiety binders.
- Fusion and emotional cut-off are often two sides of the same coin—contrasting symptoms of poorly differentiated emotional systems. Define these concepts and clarify them through examples in the texts and films that we've studied.
- Friedman asserts, "Bowen's multi-generational transmission concept is rooted in the notion that all generations are part of a continuous natural process with each generation pressing up against the next, so that the past and the present almost become a false dichotomy." What does he mean by this? Using the literature and the films we've studied, illustrate this concept.

These kinds of group activities allowed students to collaborate, as we had done, and to explicate the theory with specific examples.

By the end of the second week of class, students were asked to write their own application essays, using even more specific topics to force them deeper into the theory. For instance, one of the many complicated topics from which they could choose asked: "Track the level of chronic anxiety in *The Glass Menagerie*, scene by scene, or an in-depth analysis of the chronic anxiety in one of the scenes. Determine the level of differentiation, fusion, and/or conflict; the source of chronic anxiety; and the way the characters cope with that anxiety through over/under functioning, binding of anxiety, or shifting anxiety to a third party."

Viewing films and reading literature provided a relatively safe perspective within which to explore the family system. In many ways, it is easier to explore the artistically created family than one's own family of origin. It is less threatening and more possible to objectively view the unfolding emotional patterns, thematic legacies, chronic anxiety, and the complex process of differentiation through fiction and cinema. What was (and is) fascinating for us as instructors is that without formal study in family systems theory, exceptional writers and directors display remarkable compassion for and insight into universal family functioning.

In addition, the genograms and family biographies moved the learning from the more objective and abstract to the more subjective and personal, where students could more easily articulate inside and outside positions in triangles, clearly discuss the role of over-functioning and under-functioning in symptom development, and distinguish between the nature of functional and basic differentiation in a fictional family. Once students began focusing on their own multi-generational families, objectivity melted away, and their clarity of thinking became blurred with emotional reactivity and chronic anxiety.

Nonetheless, having learned the central theoretical elements in Bowen theory, students were poised to use their own families as laboratories for personal exploration, investigation, and understanding. In particular, the genogram presentations created a depth of compassion, insight, and awareness that was almost unparalleled in both instructors' years of teaching. The presentations became a mechanism to apply what we were learning and a venue to share familial secrets, hopes, and fears from the past and for the future. Truly, the developmental sequence of intellectual understanding through fictional families and personalization of the theory through the genogram and subsequent family biography assignments grounded the students learning in powerful ways.

Modifications and Adjustments

Despite its initial success, we realized that there were significant areas in need of modification and adjustment for the second offering of the course. In the first incarnation, for example, we allowed the students a lot of flexibility and input into the design of the course. Students not only presented their individual genograms, which took, much to our surprise, an entire week of a four-week class, but we also allowed them to choose films for us to watch as a group and stories for us to read.

Uncharacteristically, for the second offering, we modified and adjusted the course by limiting student participation in film selection. We normally provide ample opportunity for students to help develop the syllabus and the course; however, the films the students selected the first time lacked internal systemic consistency or provided only marginal opportunities to integrate theoretical analysis with artistic critique.

In addition, during the first course offering, we had given over the last week of class to collaborative presentations of students' creative application assignments. Group topics included family systems applied to art therapy, improvisational theatre, and even the multigenerational history of elephant families in South Africa. In some ways, this collaboration with other students was effective. Students felt greater ownership of the course, and it did significantly broaden the scope and the application of the theory to other disciplines. We felt, however, that we had given over almost half of the course to the students, and that we had sacrificed depth of understanding of the theory as well as practice with application of the theory in both clinical and literary/cinematic contexts.

We determined that in an interdisciplinary course, students must struggle to integrate the two disciplines. In order to facilitate their understanding, it is important for us, as instructors, to provide greater structure and create more focused assignments. We were wary this time about relinquishing so much autonomy to the students in designing projects that ranged too far from the already complicated work we were doing. As a result, in the second version of the course, we actually increased the size of our reader, adding more theoretical material on Bowen Family Systems Theory as well as additional literary texts. We also modified the film list to better represent the cinematic family and theoretical components of the theory. We replaced *Grand Canyon* and *Hamlet* with *American Beauty*, *Godfather I* and *Godfather II*, while keeping *Life Lessons*, *What's Eating Gilbert Grape*, *The Glass Menagerie*, and *Hanna and Her Sisters*.

We streamlined our assignments, providing more opportunities for students to digest the theory and begin applying it to both film and literature in full-class settings as well as in small groups. As a result, their major application essays demonstrated greater depth and analytical sophistication. We kept the student genogram work and presentations but set tighter limitations on presentation time. We also maintained the outside fieldtrip components of the class. The first time we taught the course, these fieldtrips were successful in generating a sense of group cohesion, and we wanted to replicate this success. We agreed as a class to see a current movie, *The Royal Tenenbaums*, which had just been released at the theatre, and we saw a regional theatre one-man show, focusing on a Latin-American family. We supplemented the course with an all-day Italian pasta party, where we watched and analyzed the first two films of *The Godfather* series.

We deleted the collaborative presentation assignment and replaced it with two other assignments that more directly related to the content of the course. The first was a family biography/family systems analysis, where students were able to put in narrative form their genogram work, first describing and then examining a family theme, multi-generational pattern, interconnected pattern, central emotional triangle, or family secret in their own families:

> **Family Secret.** According to the theory, there are no secrets in a family. The entire system colludes in keeping them. In many of the films and literature we studied, as well as the genogram presentations, you've seen how secrets can be transmitted through generations. Often these secrets are linked powerfully to the family's conception of shame and may be used as a tool for one generation to exert its will (about how to behave properly or ethically) over another generation. For example, in the families we've studied in class, suppression of a Chinese woman's story creates anxiety in her niece, who searches desperately for "ancestral help"; a suicide is covered up to protect the children; a priest and a baroness produce an illegitimate child. Is there a secret in your own family? How has that secret generated chronic anxiety in your family's emotional system? Can you identify the members of the family throughout the generations who bind the anxiety of this suppressed secret? How do they bind it? What is the effect of the secret on the functional differentiation of the members of the family?

This assignment, in effect, allowed students to create a piece of literature—their family story or myth—and then to analyze that narrative using the theory.

The final assignment was a take-home exam that allowed students to demonstrate their understanding of the seminal concepts of Bowen Family Systems Theory, using at least three assigned texts or stories that we *hadn't* discussed in class. The second part of the exam allowed students a tremendous amount of leeway. They could write a story, a short memoir, a series of poems, a song, or create a visual collage or series of paintings or photographs, a game for the class, a performance piece, or any other creative means of demonstrating their personalization of the theory.

These final two assignments—the family biography/analysis and the exam—worked especially well. Both assignments allowed students to personalize their learning and to have greater autonomy, characteristics we didn't want to lose from the first class. The assignments, though, were more directly related to the already complicated subject matter of this course and allowed the students opportunities to deepen their analysis and synthesis skills.

When we taught the course for the second time in the winter of 2002, it was over-enrolled with a waiting list. We felt pleased by the word-of-mouth generated by the first class. Most of the students were juniors and seniors this second time around, which helped with the pace of the class, as we were able to proceed quickly through introductory material and gear the class to the high functioning level of the group.

With one class cycle under our belts, we felt more comfortable with the material and with the modifications and adjustments to the structure and content of the course. *The Godfather* marathon was especially effective and engaging. This day-long film festival was intense, as the films, while brilliant, are violent and disturbing and provided a wonderful opportunity for group cohesiveness through cooking, eating, and learning together.

The changes we made contributed to the increased success. We had streamlined the course and tightened our reading and writing requirements, provided opportunities for field trips, and class retreats, and flexibility to meet student interest. Once again, students embraced the opportunity to construct their family genograms and present them to the class. As instructors, we set reasonable but firm limits for class presentation of genograms. Knowing that they each had twenty minutes to present their genograms and receive feedback, student presentations were much more focused than the first time. Not surprisingly, we found that teaching the class a second time was more effective. Our confidence working as an interdisciplinary team and our comfort with the material and each other's style allowed for greater flow and, perhaps most importantly (from a Bowen theory perspective), we felt less anxiety and thus generated less anxiety in the class. In essence, we had more fun and students perceived us as more relaxed and (ironically, given our tightening of the structure) more flexible with assignments. We discovered that by creating more structure for the class, we did a better job of unleashing our students' potential. Their course evaluations and end-of-year-debriefs revealed that they seemed happier and better served as well.

While we will no doubt make adjustments for the next incarnation of the course, we believe that we have finally found an essentially balanced course design that allows students to become literate in these two fields of study, to demonstrate their growing mastery of methodology, and to apply and personalize their learning.

Interdisciplinary Team Teaching: Reflections and Suggestions

Working with a colleague from another discipline can be an incredibly rewarding experience. For us, the experience enriched both our personal friendship and our professional lives. For example, Kenny's appreciation for and understanding of Bowen theory grew tremendously. He embraced Bowen theory not simply for its application to film and literature but for its usefulness as a theoretical system in his current leadership role as the Associate Dean of the Resident Degree Program at Prescott College. He finds the theory applicable and invaluable as he manages the many day-to-day requirements of his job and for long-term planning and development. Wayne has found that he approaches film and literature with a greater understanding of form and aesthetics, and he has learned not only to see systems in these creative expressions but also to appreciate how writers, directors, and screenwriters approach their craft. This understanding and appreciation has also helped him expand his professional commitment to Bowen theory beyond the family system into artistic expression, leadership, education, and macro-systems.

Based on our experiences, we offer these four central suggestions for faculty interested in team teaching an interdisciplinary course or administrators interested in fostering an interdisciplinary curriculum:

I. Interdisciplinary Pollination: Choosing Disciplines to Integrate

First, it is important to distinguish between the team-taught course, in which two instructors in essentially the same discipline collaborate, and interdisciplinary team teaching, in which faculty from different disciplines work together for interdisciplinary pollination.

For example, at Prescott College, we have a heavy field curriculum, so safety issues often require the institution to provide two instructors for a course. Adventure Education is an eighteen-credit, eleven-week course in which two faculty members from our *Adventure Education* program work with ten students in the field on theory, history, practical application, and development of technical skills. In-town courses, however, may also benefit from faculty collaboration. Wayne, for instance, regularly team-teaches Community Mediation with another Human Development faculty member, who is also a trained mediator. Because mediation and conflict resolution require significant role-playing to develop basic skills, there is a strong justification for this course being taught by two faculty members, in this case one trained originally as a psychologist and systems theorist and the other as a social worker. Kenny had previously co-taught a course entitled *Travel Writing: Journey as Metaphor*. While this course took place in the field and consequently required two instructors for safety reasons, it also helped that the other instructor was a literature teacher as well as a poet, which complemented Kenny's training in literature and fiction writing. While both instructors were English teachers and writers, their different skills helped broaden the scope of the course and the student opportunities.

A truly interdisciplinary course is one in which the faculty members come from completely different academic disciplines. The course is designed to explore the intellectual and creative space that arises when you integrate the two disciplines. Other examples of this kind of course at Prescott College include *Religion and Science*, taught by a religion and philosophy professor and a geologist, and *Nature and Psyche*, taught by a conservation biologist and a counselor. In the case of *Family Systems in Film & Literature*, we were intrigued by the very different ways we examined human behavior, in particular family dynamics. As a systems practitioner and professor, Wayne brought a highly sophisticated theoretical and clinical apparatus to his understanding of family functioning. As a fiction writer and literature and creative writing professor, Kenny applied a more intuitive method to his examination of family structure and dynamics, informed by the rich literary tradition, ranging from the Greek tragedians and Shakespeare to modern and contemporary storytellers like Tennessee Williams, William Faulkner, Gabriel Garcia Marquez, and Jane Smiley.

We believed that co-teaching which combined our different

approaches would be mutually beneficial not only for our own professional growth but for our students as well. For example, one of the potential limitations of a family systems course is that there is no easy pedagogical way to examine family functioning. The work is clinical in nature, but the instructor is forced to rely on case studies, heavy theoretical immersion, and a rigorous analysis of one's own family of origin. While this kind of clinical focus obviously works, literature and film provided a relatively unexplored laboratory for analysis of family functioning, as well as a way of at least informally testing the theory. That is, if the theory does indeed have universal applications as it purports, then the analysis should hold up just as well for a classic text of family functioning, such as *Hamlet*, as it will for a contemporary clinical situation.

Similarly, for literature, writing, and film students, this course would give students a critical lens and theoretical vocabulary by which to examine not only the imaginative narratives of classic and contemporary texts but also their own lives. Often a film, literature, or creative writing course is concerned with form and aesthetics. This kind of approach allows literature students an opportunity to step outside their roles as aesthetic or cultural critics and explore in more depth the psychological issues of a text and the way the characters may clarify and illustrate the complexities of theory. To date, most psychological studies in literature and film have used Freudian or Jungian approaches. A family systems model provides a fresh approach to psycho-literary studies.

The pitfall of such an interdisciplinary approach is that it can potentially subvert the intentions of both disciplines. Both psychology and literature students may begin to see the characters in a play or novel or film as clinical patients, in need of diagnoses and counseling, rather than as imaginary figures functioning within a larger ritual of form: tragedy, comedy, romance, naturalism, absurdism, etc. If the artist has done his or her job right, then the characters should live and breathe and provide insight into the complexities, frailties, and foibles of human behavior. The writer or director's goal is not to present a case study; however, we sought to examine this very complexity. Human behavior is never neat. Intelligent and good-intentioned people cannot be easily reduced. Differentiation, chronic anxiety, multigenerational transmission process. . . these are all qualitative assessments that involve some degree of inference once you apply them to either real or imaginary people. We were convinced that the theory would activate our students' curiosity about the intellectual implications of narratives while the literature and films would humanize the theory, thus making it accessible.

Our suggestion to prospective interdisciplinary team-teachers? Choose the disciplines to combine carefully. Make sure that the integration stretches you and the students beyond your comfort zones but that the disciplines also effectively illuminate and deepen the understanding of each other.

II. Narrow the Focus

It is important to find a balance between breadth and depth. Remember that the primary goal of an interdisciplinary course is to examine the area *between* the disciplines rather than try to fully articulate both. In our initial plan for the course, this was one of the major obstacles we confronted. Our original course title was *Family Systems in Film*. However, we felt that by limiting our "laboratory" to just film, we would be eliminating great resources. Film, like drama, is primarily an external medium. The narrative unfolds almost exclusively through action and dialogue. In fiction, poetry, and narrative nonfiction, the narrative often unfolds *internally*; reflection, lyrical meditation, analysis of character and situation are just as crucial, if not more so, as dialogue and action. We wanted this double vision. We also wanted to examine a case study of a writer, to show the evolution of a family story in different mediums. This wider focus allowed us, for example, to explore Tennessee Williams' autobiographical family drama, *The Glass Menagerie*. We were able to read about Williams' own family history and see how he transformed that history first into a short story, "A Portrait of a Girl in Glass," then into his acclaimed play, and finally to see how that play is realized in a production by a sensitive director and skilled actors (in this case the filmed adaptation directed by Paul Newman).

While this broadening of our scope was initially liberating, we still struggled early on with the problem of having too much material to cover in too short a period of time—a four-week, intensive block session. At first, we felt that we needed to serve our respective constituents: psychology versus writing and literature students. There were complex learning outcomes that were expected in a straightforward family systems course. Those students needed a solid grounding in the clinical applications of family systems theory. Similarly, writing, literature, and film students were expected to hone and deepen their understanding of literary and cinematic theory. Could we accomplish both objectives in this course without subverting our original goal? Something had to give.

We agreed that depth was more important that breadth. We would both have to compromise in order to achieve our larger goal. As described earlier, we determined that the course needed to be primarily a family systems course. The literature and films should be used to explicate and clarify the theory while also allowing us opportunities to examine the subtle complexities of family functioning. We decided that, first and foremost, we needed to ground students in the theory, and then to let them deepen their understanding by applying what they had learned not only to the texts and films we were watching and reading in class, but also to their own lives. Once we agreed on this central objective, we were able to structure the course easily, breaking it into three overarching teaching imperatives: (1) Introduction to Key Issues & Concepts; (2) Application to Literature/Film/Our Lives; and (3) Synthesis and Conclusions.

III. Administrative Considerations: Prerequisites, Curricular Justification, and Workload Issues

In addition to the pedagogical logistics we were trying to work out with each other, we also had to contend, as all team teachers must, with significant administrative issues. We had to, in other words, sell our course to the administration, to justify it both curricularly and financially.

One of the minor, though still important, administrative issues that every interdisciplinary course must confront is what level of students to pitch the course to and what prerequisites to require. We designed this course for upper-division students. We wanted to emphasize and help students hone sophisticated analysis and synthesis skills. Yet, we also wanted to attract psychology as well as literature and writing students. We knew that the chances were slim that any student would have significant coursework in psychology, literature, creative writing, and film. Here again, we compromised. If this class was to be a true interdisciplinary think tank, then our students would be very much like us: they would probably have significant academic training in one area or the other. We decided to require all students to have at least freshman composition and *either* significant coursework in psychology/human development or literature, creative writing, or film studies. This decision turned out to be fortuitous since we attracted students from across the college, and they each brought special expertise to the content area, but the course also stretched everyone's intellectual and creative muscles as well; like us, no one had tried to link these two disciplines together in any systematic or rigorous way, nor had they explored the potential benefits of such an integration.

In addition to creating prerequisites that would effectively attract a wider spectrum of upper-division students, we also needed to make a curricular case for our course. We had to make sure it served both student constituents in their major or minor areas of focus. We believe that any interdisciplinary course must address this larger institutional necessity in order to succeed. Toward this end, Wayne proposed that the Human Development/Psychology advising document allow our course to substitute for the more clinical *Family Systems Theory* course. Kenny worked with his writing and literature colleagues to adopt a new literature requirement—Cross-Disciplinary Literature, which included courses such as *American West in Film and Literature, Holy Books, Philosophies of the Interpretive Naturalists*, and *Women's Literature*—that all Writing and Literature students would need to fulfill.

Perhaps the most demanding administrative hurdle that team teachers must overcome is convincing department chairs and deans that the allocation of resources is worth the cost. At Prescott College, we were in the fortunate position of serving as the dean and the program chair during the time when we presented our course for approval. Regardless, we are fortunate at Prescott College that all classes have an average college-wide 10:1 student/faculty ratio. Already, this low ratio creates a risky cost-benefit analysis for our administration. When you factor in field courses, which often require double staffing and can drive the ratio down to as low as 4:1, then the prospect of allowing two faculty members to co-teach an in-town, upper-division course can seem highly suspect, if not downright insane, from a budgetary standpoint. It's even more crucial, in these circumstances, to create prerequisites that allow students from across the college to participate, and for both instructors to build consensus in their respective curricular areas or programs so that students have an advising incentive to take the course. It also helps if you can acquire outside funding. For example, the instructors for Prescott College's *Religion and Science* course applied for and received a sizable outside grant to help fund their own research and to reward Prescott College financially for supporting such interdisciplinary ventures. While we have not applied for such funding, we have compromised by increasing our course capacity and by offering the course on a rotating basis every two years so that the impact on both our teaching loads is significantly reduced.

While Prescott College generally supports this interdisciplinary team teaching approach, the institution does impose some general limitations on this work. For one, each instructor can only team-teach once a year. This limit helps ensure balance and curricular continuity. Second, the college has instituted a Number of Students Served (NSS) system to monitor faculty workload and help ensure equality and balance from all faculty members. Team teaching only credits the faculty with .67 NSS for every student enrolled, rather than the normal 1.0 NSS for each student enrolled in an in-town class. This "reduced credit" also encourages us to expand enrollment caps for our class or to increase our other class loads. In effect, the college still needs to manage its curriculum with limited resources and limited faculty.

IV. Communication: Preparation, Planning, and Student Assignments

The central myth to dispel when considering team teaching is that it requires less work. After all, with two people teaching the same course, shouldn't the workload be lessened? Unfortunately, the opposite is true. Given the nature of collaboration, the differences in personality and teaching styles, and the complexity of the interdisciplinary material, this kind of team teaching requires more time, more preparation, and more coordination than teaching alone. For *Family Systems in Film & Literature*, the one exception was with reading, correcting, and critiquing student assignments. The first time that we taught the class, we each read, corrected, and critiqued all of the students' papers. In part, this was due to our lack of familiarity with each other's style and critiquing methods. Being committed "over-functioners" with a penchant for academic rigor, however, we soon realized that much of our reviews and critiques were redundant. The second time that we taught the class, we divided the student assignments, making sure that we both worked with each student for at least one significant writing assignment.

Even with this splitting of the student written workload, interdisciplinary team teaching remains a time-intensive commitment. In addition, it functions best when the instructors can check their egos at the door. Fortunately, we have developed enough confidence as teachers to allow each other plenty of leeway in the classroom. At times, Kenny will direct the class, explicating a text or providing the literary or historical context for a film. At other times, Wayne's clarification on a theoretical concept will take center stage. Sometimes, these presentations are planned; other times, they occur spontaneously from teachable moments. We keep in close contact with each other, with daily discussions before and after class to ensure balance, comfort, and class continuity. In addition, we keep in regular and close contact with the students, ensuring that their needs are being appropriately considered and to monitor and adjust based on their feedback.

Any team-taught course requires a tremendous amount of communication and trust. Rarely, especially in the initial conception and design of the course, does it involve less work. We had been discussing the possibility of teaching *Family Systems in Film & Literature* for six years before we actually were able to teach it. Once the course was approved and in the curriculum, our planning was extensive. We both had to master, to some extent, each other's discipline. We had to learn to speak each other's professional language. We had to remember that it was okay to ask dumb questions. Our collaboration humbled us in important ways that we believe benefited our students and our teaching for this and other courses. We were reminded of both the thrill and the struggle of having a beginner's mind. Also, because we had just struggled to learn the material, once the course began, we felt more empathy for our students' struggles to digest the material and their ability to integrate the disciplines effectively. We also felt a great deal of pride in them since we knew how difficult the task that we set was.

The primary piece of advice we offer is to double whatever amount of time you think you need to prepare the course. We discovered that it was essential to more fully prepare this course than either of us was accustomed to doing with our own courses. Collaboration depended on good planning, both for the overall design and the day-by-day classes. Paradoxically, we needed to know more so that we could feel comfortable improvising. One of the payoffs for this kind of intense preparation was that we got to learn how the other person taught. Teaching is, ironically, a rather solitary act, especially at the college or university level. There's not much oversight, and faculty are generally given a great deal of autonomy. The down side is that we rarely get an opportunity to discuss and learn, in a detailed way, how our colleagues actually do what they do. In this kind of team teaching situation, you get that opportunity, and it can't help but enrich your own teaching to see how another professor designs a course, prepares for class, improvises from the plan, and responds to the inevitable teaching moments that arise every day. It was truly inspiring for us both—not just as scholars being allowed to learn a new discipline but also as teachers engaged in an on-going pedagogical colloquium.

Conclusion: Differentiated Teaching

Should differentiated teaching be a goal? We are teaching the course for the third time this fall°. We've both certainly become more adept. We've learned to trust each other with the material. Kenny has no qualms about turning over a literary or film analysis to Wayne, and Wayne regularly lets Kenny explicate the theory. We've both grown immensely. For Kenny, his deepening understanding of the theory has benefited him not only as a literary and film critic, but also as a writer, administrator, and person. Wayne uses film and literature more fully in his own family systems classes and also teaches a systems approach to leadership, which draws on our working conversations and our collaborations in the classroom. He's a closer examiner of texts and films, and now he has a useful tool for illustrating complex human interactions in a clinical setting.

Could either of us teach the course alone? Perhaps. But we won't do that, nor should it really be the goal for any genuinely interdisciplinary course. In an interdisciplinary team-teaching situation, the source of both intellectual and creative energy is the exploration of the space between disciplines, and it helps to have two people bringing their different professional lenses to bear on the subject matter. We hope this kind of learning environment serves as a model for our students of the kind of work we'd like them to aspire to at Prescott College: work where intellectual boundaries are permeable rather than rigid, where collaboration is encouraged rather than academically suspect, and where they can apply and personalize theoretical material, moving beyond analysis and evaluation to the truly creative realm of synthesis. Our experiences have taught us that interdisciplinary team teaching can be—if academically nourished, rigorously conceived, and effectively executed—liberal arts education at its best.

° Essay originally written in the summer of 2003

LIZ FALLER

*One of the most enticing aspects of experiential education is the
potential for service-based projects. Students move beyond simply
putting education into practice and actually affect change. In this essay,
Liz Faller vividly recounts one such project and the effects it had on both
the community and the students.*

*"The Dance for Wildernees Project served as an excellent vehicle for
interdisciplinary, service-based, experiential education," she says,
"integrating our curricular programs—including Environmental Studies,
Arts and Letters, Integrative Studies, and Adventure Education."*

*Liz Faller's thirty years experience in dance, performance,
production, community organization, and environmental activism have
led her to dance in such diverse places as Africa, Bali, Belize, Mexico, and
Thailand. Since 1993, she has been an instructor in Arts & Letters and in
Human Development at Prescott College.*

THE DANCE FOR WILDERNESS PROJECT:
INTERDISCIPLINARY, SERVICE-BASED EDUCATION

"Throughout this project I learned to see celebration as a form of activism
and compassion as a catalyst for change."

-Catlin Smith (student)

In the fall semester of 2002, Prescott College offered an experimental
three-course, pilot project titled *Dance for Wilderness*. The primary
goal was to elevate public awareness of the beauty and importance of
Desolation Canyon, Utah, through a performance art tribute.

Rachel Peters, Prescott College's Field Support and Permit
Coordinator and Dennis Willis of the Price, Utah, Bureau of Land
Management (BLM) office conceived the project. Since Prescott College
classes have rafted and studied this remote and awe-inspiring canyon on
the Green River for over thirty years, Peters wanted to find a way for the
college to give back to the canyon. Willis wanted something unique that
would provide outreach, connection with community, and communication
of the beauty of Desolation Canyon. Because of its educational
philosophy and focus on the liberal arts, Willis invited the college to
"dance the canyon" for the community.

Rachel Peters sought members of the faculty and administration she

knew would be excited by such an opportunity and challenge, inviting
me, a performing arts instructor, and Bob Ellis, an environmental studies
professor, to head the project. We were both passionately involved in
related work and shared a lively interest in one another's field of
expertise. In fact, we had been discussing the importance of bringing
together the performing arts and environmental studies for several
years. I had been teaching *Nature and Dance* for seven years and am
an experienced community organizer. Bob previously lived in Utah, is a
wilderness advocate, and has an ongoing relationship with the canyon.

After interviewing qualified students and gaining administrative
support, we designed three special topics courses in wilderness
designation, interdisciplinary performance, and student-selected
independent studies. In their independent studies, students would
work with faculty in several programs including Journalism and Eco-
psychology to augment their studies. Eleven dancers enthusiastically
committed themselves to the project—the opportunity to merge their
love for dance, for the environment, and for community service was
especially compelling.

The ten-week course began with a ten-day raft trip through the
canyon to learn the geology, natural history, culture, and politics of the
region, and to inspire artistic expression born of profound, direct
experience. Following the raft trip, the class spent four days getting to
know the local community, hosted by a city organization, Culture
Connection, and City Council member Liz Kourianos. Stories about
experiences in Desolation Canyon and local music were gathered to
incorporate into the performance. This included numerous private
interviews, a community meeting and the ensemble's participation in an
artist salon. Upon their return to Prescott, students had less than a
month to put together the performance while continuing their studies
in wilderness designation.

The project culminated in the multi-media performance, *Hidden
Wonder of Carbon County: A Performance Art Tribute to Desolation
Canyon*. After performing for a packed and enthusiastic Prescott crowd
in late November, the class returned to Price for rehearsals and to
finalize program alterations. On December 6th, the ensemble opened
its two night showing to a diverse audience in Price. The performance
blended choreographed and improvisational dance, spoken word,
poetry, song, story, recorded music, live music (including flute, drums,
and didgeridoo), and slides of photographs and paintings.

Many questioned if a wilderness could be portrayed through a stage

performance. But Dennis Willis's comments after the performance
served as a convincing affirmation of success:

> The performance captured the rhythm and flow of a
> journey through a remarkable place. The creativity
> and presentation helped me remember some
> connections to the canyon that had evidently been
> suppressed or taken for granted after twenty-two years
> and sixty trips through the canyon.

With his invitation to dance the canyon, Willis had set up a testing
ground for our institution: a time to walk our talk, to mobilize and join
our resources, expertise, and talents for the greater good.

In our initial meetings for the project, we considered possible pitfalls
and designed the program in a way that consciously addressed our
limitations and emphasized our strengths. We prepared ourselves for a
large learning curve and rallied our senses of humor. What follows is an
informal outline of some of the key elements that played into our success:

Clear Basis of Unity

The fact that Dennis Willis of the BLM invited us to dance the
canyon provided a strong foundation from which to move. It was
important to use his intention as our core mission statement: To elevate
public awareness of the beauty and importance of Desolation Canyon.
We used this shared purpose again and again to focus our efforts. The
simplicity and clarity of our love for the land and the arts served as a
strong bridge uniting diverse groups and perspectives.

Student Involvement

Since the students were involved from the beginning of the project,
their sense of ownership was high. An application process asked them
to articulate their motivations, commitments, and suggestions. Students
were involved in all aspects of the project. Those ready for more
responsibility served in semi-professional positions including artistic co-
director and production co-facilitators.

Educational exercises cultivated and magnified their personal
interests and experience. The programming highlighted their unique
talents. Their sincere appreciation of the canyon and motivation to give
their best was impressive. This was perhaps the fundamental reason the
project succeeded. Willis said, "It was a treat to see the students
express that mix of excitement, awe, and reverence that I feel every

time I go there." Ken Larson, editor of Price's daily newspaper, *Sun Advocate*, had similar feelings: "The energy the college students brought to the stage was incredible. Their talent and enthusiasm showed through as they portrayed their interpretation of Desolation Canyon, from the forces of time, the contrasts of the canyon, erosion, and the canyon as a sanctuary... It was truly beautiful."

Personal Touch

Prescott College is known by many for being a "heart-centered" institution. Personalized, positive relationships cultivated through small class sizes and individualized advising loads are hallmarks of the college. It made sense to apply this personalized approach to the project. Serving as our liaison, Rachel Peters kept in close contact with Dennis Willis throughout the project. We regularly updated our understandings and agreements. Willis gave us a list of people to contact directly in the community. He met with me and the students to clarify his ideas and expectations for the performance.

A caring camaraderie was established with Price community members, particularly our primary support person, Liz Kourianos. She actively enlisted involvement in her community, and students developed friendships where they were lodged at Price's College of Eastern Utah. Our interest in the place and community was real and heart-felt. I engaged in lengthy discussions with Ute historian, Clifford Duncan, who became an important source of encouragement. All of this resulted in locals who were curious about what we were doing and eager to help.

Compassion and Humility

We kept reminding ourselves and others that this was a pilot project and there was much to learn. When difficulties or shortcomings surfaced, we were compassionate. We received a lot of attention, at times in the form of skepticism. The incredible humility we experienced in the canyon remained with us throughout the project, helping us relax in the face of the responsibility we felt.

Trust

Because we took the time to get to know each other, everyone involved experienced a growing trust in our collaboration. We trusted that the outcome of the project would be of service, regardless if it fell short of our greater expectations. Early on Willis told the students that this effort was an act of trust on his part because he did not understand "the creative process or technical aspects of their art." Following the performance he concluded, "My trust was not only well placed, it was repaid with interest and dividends."

College-wide Support

We reached out and received support from various departments at the college. This approach directly involved as many folks in our community as possible so awareness of the project covered the campus by word of mouth. Our Communications Manager, Karlyn Haas, played a key role in our success as she provided extensive publicity, documentation, and support throughout the project. Our deans and president attended the performance and openly expressed their support. We were all especially touched when the Dean's Office sent us a beautiful bouquet of flowers on opening night.

Environmental Studies Component

The students agreed that the combination of environmental studies and performing arts was essential for the success of the performance. In her end of term summary, Bryndl Mar spoke to the importance of learning about wilderness designation in order to bring a greater sense of purpose to her performing. Student artistic co-director Arin Willey concluded:

> I was in constant awe of all that I was learning on the river. The knowledge I gained seeped into every inch of my body and informed it how to dance the canyon. Environmental studies instilled a greater compassion and deeper relationship with the landscape, plants, animals and the diverse people who traveled through the canyon.

Multi-media and Diversified Performance

Since we expected a diverse audience, we designed a multi-media program that blended educational and entertainment elements. By including song, story, dance, music, and visual art, we offered something for everyone. Willey wrote, "We know that people learn differently, so it makes sense to include verbal and audio, visual, sensual, and kinesthetic experiences within a performance." We chose a balance between honoring the ineffable magic of performance art and articulating through spoken word and poetry. We utilized strong, as well as subtle, visual effects and poignant, as well as humorous, themes. We put significant energy into our costuming.

Most of the audience and local community had never visited Desolation Canyon, so we introduced the show with key reasons the canyon is unusual, followed by a simple invocation dance accompanied by a recording of the river. A slide show of the canyon followed, along with the story of its creation, accompanied by live flute music. The performance incorporated universal themes and symbols, as well as music and poetry by local artists. Student Andrea Flanagan wrote, "By using a broad range of creative mediums, I felt we were able to master our connection with the audience." Another student, Jo Birns, wrote, "I like the sense of completeness of expression I get from interdisciplinary and multi-media performance, the feeling that the subject has been explored from all angles."

In a popular highlight of the performance, titled Sanctuary, slides of Utah painter Serena Supplee's watercolors of the canyon were projected on a large white fabric. Dressed in flowing white, the dancers gracefully merged with the colorful images, their supple bodies disappearing into the canyon forms. The effect was so moving, audience exclamations were audible.

Universal Language in the Performing Arts

The performing arts have always been a way for humans to express their profound sense of connection with the earth. In a technological world, it is easy to lose touch with these roots. And yet, it is so natural that with a little probing of the imagination, many people do remember this intrinsic connection. Our hope was that the striking of this chord would also inspire greater stewardship of the earth, a hope mirrored in Dennis Willis's specific thoughts about Desolation Canyon and reaction to the performance: "[It] is my favorite place and all it needs from our species is a little bit of care and the patience just to let it be. One of my challenges is how to tell the story of this place without promoting it. It needs more lovers, not more tourists. You have shown me a way to do just that." The students, also, began to see the universal language their performance was speaking. Andrew Wohlsen said, "Speak to someone of environmental activism and the possibility of a defensive reaction becomes present. Speak to someone of beauty, awe, and wonder, and a common chord of the human soul is sounded."

Emergent Design in Performance

Because experiential and student-centered learning are highly valued at Prescott College, we often create a performance with more student input than is common in traditional settings. The instructor/director has a delicate position of both taking and giving leadership, of stepping in and then getting out of the way. "After experiencing the patterns and relationships within Desolation Canyon's ecosystem," said student Libby Majors, "I then had the opportunity to translate these concepts into living art."

Prescott College students are encouraged to create and refine material from their own inspirations and aesthetics in ways that are appropriate to their experience level. This requires self-awareness and honesty. This can take energy and time, especially in large ensemble pieces, but it most often results in greater creative investment and involvement from the students.

River and Canyon as Metaphor

Desolation Canyon is a vast, expansive, and humbling place. It seems fitting that the goals of our performance required us to move beyond our normal limits. Whenever we grew weary from the work, we thought about all we had received from the canyon and we found the energy to go on. Going with the flow was a common theme. In the face of challenges, we focused on the ease of the river, as it flows around the obstacles and keeps moving toward its destination.

Another consistent theme was the way being in the canyon helps one to peel away layers and get back to the basics of life. Performance art engages in a similar process. There are always formidable obstacles to face. The dance shows us the way, one breath at a time. To embody one's intentions as a dancer is an exacting and humbling task.

Documentation

This project stimulated a keen interest from many. The unlikely union of diverse institutions, communities, and individuals for a common cause was good news and was inspiring. We wanted the canyon's story to reach as many as possible for various reasons. The knowledge of Desolation Canyon's value would continue to spread. Perhaps others would be inspired to find artistic avenues for helping save the wild places of their region. And more generally, perhaps we could help generate greater faith in the ways diverse interest groups might reach out to one another.

We did our best as amateurs to video, record, and photograph the project in progress, as well as the final performance. A student, Jakob Roy, took extensive slide photos on the raft trip which were essential to introducing the canyon's magnificence to folks. Most students wrote insightful reflections on their experiences, as well as mid-term and end-of-term summary papers. Some questions for the summaries were intended to generate quotations for articles (many of which I have shared in this essay). Libby Majors, did an independent study on journalism and submitted several articles for publication. Libby also was chosen to perform her solo dance on water at a showing in Phoenix several months later. She entered the competition because of her desire for more people to know about the canyon.

Karlyn Haas interviewed faculty, staff, and students involved with the project at key points in its progression and later wrote an in-depth article on the project for our college magazine, *Transitions*.

The overwhelming post-performance sentiment was one of gratitude for such a far reaching and demanding project. Everyone clearly did their best with some of the more challenging aspects of the project. We had no doubt we had contributed greatly to public awareness concerning Desolation Canyon. Even if people were unable to attend the performances, the series of newspaper articles and the striking posters hanging around town certainly got the public's attention. As Willis pointed out, the community is now much more apt to become involved if they hear of threats to the canyon.

The Dance for Wilderness project was certainly a complex and risky endeavor. Our performing arts program is only ten years old, and we had never performed outside of our own supportive community. Price, Utah, is five hundred miles away and is not a place any of us had spent much time.

The production schedule was grueling, and our budget was minimal. Our ensemble's experience level was greatly varied; several of the students had never performed. As the performing arts instructor and director, I oversaw the entire production, performance, promotion, and documentation demands with the help of the three student assistants: Willey, Mar, and Burhop. In a more ideal scenario, we would have additional lead-time to set up budgetary, scheduling, and staffing needs. We would have more production and technical support assistance. There needs to be a minimal of two performing arts faculty involved, as well as a technical crew. It is also important to include the post-project needs of documentation and continued outreach in the design.

Much was at stake. With increased use of the rivers and limited permitting, it is more difficult to acquire permits. Current systems recognize educational institutions as commercial entities doing business on public lands, putting us in heavy competition for maintaining our unique relationship with the rivers. This project gave us an opportunity to prove that educational institutions have something special to offer to governing agencies, to local communities, and perhaps to the land itself. Rachel Peters writes:

> New and increasing demands on our river resources (namely recreation and ecosystem management) coupled with thin budgets and overworked staff, have prompted agencies to be more creative as they do the work of conservation. Meanwhile, progressive academic institutions have embraced new and innovative approaches to education that emphasize experiential, project-based learning that make tangible, positive contributions to society. Academic institutions can offer new ideas, expertise, and support for important agency projects. Agencies and academic institutions are crafting new partnerships to meet the new challenges of conservation. Successful partnerships are often bioregionally based and build on the strengths of each partner. They include clear expectations and time frames, and they remain focused on benefiting the natural resources and communities.

It's exciting to consider the possibilities of continuing to develop such innovative partnerships. The collaborations between diverse programs provide a wealth of experience that more closely reflect the real challenges and opportunities of our world today. Students involved in the *Dance for Wilderness* project often spoke to the ways the project was helping to prepare them for the complexities of the future.

Elevating public awareness of wild and natural places that need protection through the arts could be a worthy long-term commitment of the college, possibly offering a similar project every two or three years. It may make sense to choose wilderness areas that are closer to home, although establishing a greater sense of our bio-region is certainly valuable.

In the spring of 2004 I was invited by Albright College in Reading, PA to offer a presentation on the project. Bryndl Mar, Jason Goldberg, and I created a fifteen minute video short of the performance and with the technical support of another student, Marissa Langlais, I created a PowerPoint presentation on our *Nature and Dance* course. While at

Albright, I also taught two related courses, one in ecology & spirituality, the other in sacred dance. Many of the students had never spent significant time in the outdoors, yet the discussions and interactive exercises that followed were thoughtful and provocative. One faculty member even commented on how focused and engaged the students were during the presentation and classes.

Where we will go from here is yet to be seen. We will need to continue addressing the challenges of setting up interdisciplinary projects within a system that is primarily set up for individualized courses and programs. We were fortunate that the college was flexible enough to support such a spontaneous and timely project. The question remains how to include similar endeavors in the future. Creating a curriculum that provides space for multi-program, project-based education with current special topics will require considerable creative planning. *The Dance for Wilderness* project certainly demonstrated the value of making such an effort.

DAVID GILLIGAN

In "Life in the Rise," David Gilligan takes us on the journey of a field-based natural history and ecology course as they ascend the west slope of the Sierra Nevada. Along the way, we see what students learn on a course like this, how they learn it, and why it's so important that they learn it outside, in the field, firsthand.

"So much of what we do happens in the field," says Gilligan. "Often, people who don't have such opportunities have no concept of what happens out there. Hopefully, this will give them a glimpse."

David Gilligan is a member of the Adventure Education faculty at Prescott College and the author of The Secret Sierra: The Alpine World Above the Trees.

LIFE ON THE RISE

In the sweltering heat of a California summer, I set out from the floor of Kings Canyon to simulate a journey to the Arctic. With me were seven seasoned students. As scholars of natural history and ecology, these seven had long since heard of the idea that going up the mountain is like going north. Now was their chance to experience this firsthand. We had been in the backcountry together for over two weeks already— part of a ten week Prescott College field quarter studying natural history and ecology in the mountains of California. Our bodies were becoming accustomed to the rigors of life in the field and the strain of carrying everything we needed for eleven days in the mountains. Our noses were burnt and peeled, calves taut; we knew what each other liked to eat, what each other smelled like, who stayed up late, who slept in, who was the turtle, and who was the hare. Laden with necessities and strengthened by some experience, we set out across the hot, dusty, pine-scented flats of the canyon. Thoughts of cool alpine meadows and crunchy snowfields gave meaning to the sweat that soaked our packs as they pressed into our backs; we knew well the toll that nine-thousand vertical feet would take on our legs before we would ever reach such high places.

Roam where you will in the wrinkled mountain landscape of California, and you will find more species of plants and animals than occur in any similar-sized chunk of land in temperate North America, if not the world. Over five thousand species of native plants occur here,

115

over half of which occur nowhere else in the world. There are lush forests of redwoods, dry oak savannahs, parched grasslands, sun drenched deserts, fertile ribbons of streamside woodland, stately conifer forests, and windswept expanses of alpine tundra. The synopsis of all this is that diverse topography means diverse habitats, and diverse habitats means more species.

Early explorers and geographers, and perhaps even their far-reaching stone-age predecessors, found that they could predict, with a reasonable degree of success, the types of landscapes they would encounter on their travels. It was no mystery that the equatorial regions were warm, even hot, while the polar regions were bitterly cold. Everything in between, whether traveling north or south from the equator, became increasingly cooler the farther one traveled.

Explorers discovered many things (often the hard way) that today we take for granted as common knowledge. In the tropics they encountered dense jungles of rainforests, often impenetrable, crawling with insects, ornate birds, and vocal monkeys. Diversity among species here was extraordinary. In search of fabled cities of gold, they tore deep into the hot, humid, green realms of Central and South America. In analogous equatorial regions of sub-Saharan Africa, Southeast Asia, and Oceana they found the same types of landscapes. The particular species may have differed considerably, but the climatic conditions, the soils, the structure and functions of the flora and fauna were the same. Traveling north, the trend continued. Deserts dominated the subtropical arid regions in latitudes of twenty to forty degrees north and south, including the Sahara, the Australian, the Arabian, the Sonoran, the Chihuahuan, the Atacama. The species of plants and animals varied from place to place, but the climatic conditions, soils, and adaptations plants used to cope with these physical factors were the same. In temperate latitudes, where storms were more common and moisture was adequate, forests grew, cloaking most of Europe, Asia, and much of North America. These temperate forests were deciduous in areas with consistent year-round moisture, coniferous in areas that experienced dry times. Where pronounced dry seasons occurred, expansive grasslands replaced the trees, as we see in the steppes of Eurasia, the Great Plains of North America, and California's Central Valley. Further north, in latitudes that came to be known as the roaring forties and furious fifties, where the growing season was shortened and snow covered the ground for much of the year, the forests changed dramatically. Here, conifers ruled, conical and flexible to shed snow, evergreen to take advantage of short warm

116

spells and get a head start on summer. A few notable exceptions to the evergreen rule made a living in these boreal forests of the north: fluttering aspens, bright paper birches, chaste alders and willows. Overall, however, diversity of species was low, though the numbers of individuals of the same species overwhelming. Still further north, above sixty degrees, the storm systems settled down considerably, but the growing season temperatures were so cold that the trees stopped growing altogether. Permafrost crept into the ground. Beneath the mysterious green warping skies of aura borealis and the amber light of the midnight sun, the trees gave way to vast tundra: an elaborate system of bogs, meadows, and fellfields extending into the high arctic. Eventually even these prostrate plants couldn't make it, and only a few tenacious lichens survived in the extreme polar regions.

Later, research in the fields of climatology, soil science, ecology, and geography confirmed what had been speculated for so long. Maps generated from all of these disparate branches of science illustrated the same basic point: Although climate, vegetation, and soils all influence each other, climate is the ultimate arbiter of the geography of life and soils. Climate, of course, as demonstrated by the findings of the early explorers, is strongly dictated by latitude.

The ecologist Paul Colinvaux identifies eight terrestrial biomes (vegetation formations delineated by geography): arctic tundra, boreal forest, temperate forest, temperate grassland, chaparral, desert, tropical savannah, and tropical rainforest. If you were to walk a straight line from the central coast of California to the Nevada border, you would boast of having seen six (arguably seven) of the eight terrestrial biomes of the world. There is no place else in North America, and few places in the world, where you could make such a boast. Pick just about any one spot on the globe and you will find one or two, rarely three, of these eight biomes represented. Alaska has arctic tundra, boreal forest, and arguably some temperate forest in the southeast. Equatorial Africa has tropical savannah and tropical rainforest. Siberia has only boreal forest. Australia, an entire continent, is predominantly desert with smaller areas of temperate forest and grassland on the eastern seaboard and tropical rainforest along the north coast. To find a place where the most biomes are represented in the smallest area, you need either to pick a long, skinny piece of land with a vast latitudinal span (such as Chile in South America), or find a place where a wide latitudinal range is simulated by a wide range of elevation. To do that, you need mountains.

It had long been known that going up a mountain is like traveling north, but it was not until the late nineteenth century that the naturalist C. Hart Merriam consolidated and published his lifezone theory to explain it. The short version is that temperature decreases with elevation, now quantified at a rate of three to 5.5 degrees Fahrenheit for every thousand feet, depending on the relative humidity of the air mass. Not by mere coincidence, precipitation rates increase with elevation. This means mountains are colder and wetter than the surrounding lowlands, thus simulating more northerly climes. Going up a mountain one thousand feet is like going north two hundred miles.

Nowhere in the contiguous United States is the idea of elevation simulating latitude more drastic, more stunning, than in the canyon of the Kings River. Here, the waters of the south-central Sierra Nevada gather from the highest snow-encrusted peaks and ridges and cut down through the landscape in an incessant quest for the sea. Nine thousand feet of elevation are spanned by the walls of the canyon, from the chilling alpine heights at fourteen-thousand feet, to the warm pine woodlands and chaparral of the canyon bottom at five-thousand feet. The Kings is deeper than Grand Canyon, and in contrast to its southwestern counterpart, to look in you must climb up to its rims, to the skyscraping granite tops of innumerable mountains.

From an ecological perspective, walking the nine-thousand vertical feet from the canyon floor to the surrounding summits is like walking one-thousand eight-hundred miles north. On such a lengthy northerly sojourn, you would pass through semi-arid conifer woodlands laced with lush riparian gallery forests, interspersed with open grassland and temperate savannah, shrubby chaparral, cold sagebrush desert, sweet-smelling pine forests, well-ordered boreal forests, and finally, the windswept expanse of the arctic tundra. You would end your journey after months, if not years, of traveling to tell the tale that going north it gets colder, the weather changes, and the plants and the soils they grow upon change correspondingly. You would be standing on the permanently frozen soils of the Yukon Plateau, perhaps looking up at a shimmering display of aura borealis and settling in for a night of sub-polar slumber as the mercury dropped to fifty degrees below zero. Or, you could spend just a few days walking in Kings Canyon and see much the same things.

After a long walk across the flat-bottomed valley of the Kings River, we ascended Bubbs Creek drainage, trudging up steep switchbacks on a hot and dry southwest slope. It was a textbook situation. Here were woodland and chaparral species, species that Merriam would have called Upper Sonoran, growing higher than the lower montane transition zone species of the valley floor, where cold air pools regularly every night. We passed canyon live oaks, bush chinquapin, manzanita, whitethorn, and even a stray pinyon, leaving drops of sweat on their parched leaf surfaces. As we reached the top of the slope, we tucked into the valley of Bubbs Creek, noticing gigantic sugar pine cones littering the forest floor as the forest trees of the transition zone thankfully closed in around us.

Continuing upward, we found ourselves once again pounded by the midday sun as we plodded up the rocky switchbacks along Sphinx Creek. The terrain was typical of the Sierra Nevada: flat treads of valley walking—characterized by meandering or rushing streams and placid lakes—interspersed with huge steep risers of bare granite and plummeting waterfalls. This was the glacial staircase, an undulating stair-step topography fit for the most giant of giants, which we would follow to its uppermost summit. The valley of the Kings loomed large and far away, now three thousand feet below us, with its forest dark green and thick. Eventually the riser bent into another tread, and we followed the less hurried Sphinx Creek into its sheltered drainage. Tucked away from the sun, huge trees grew, and the massive trunks of red firs and western white pines grew up to thick branches and green scented boughs. Beneath the canopy, numerous small streams intersected flowering red mountain heather and pinemat manzanita, cascading down the slope towards Sphinx Creek. Paralleling Sphinx Creek, we crossed these tributaries, one after the other, decorated with vibrant seep spring monkeyflowers, largeleaf lupines, big red paintbrushes, cinquefoils, and secretive bog orchids. This forest was decidedly more northern than the one below. At the Sphinx Creek crossing, we rested, and leaning comfortably against rocks and logs, we all spontaneously and simultaneously fell asleep. We awoke to the high wail of mosquitos. They had found us. Surely we must be in Canada.

With another thousand feet to ascend, we hoisted our ten days of food, clothing, shelter, notebooks, textbooks, ice axes, helmets, and human waste devices, and set out off-trail. We followed Sphinx Creek more closely this time, ascending yet another riser towards where we hoped we would find some slabs to camp on. Passing through forest-line, we emerged into an extensive stand of quaking aspen, leaves aflutter in the afternoon breeze. Here we paused and listened to the sound of the wind in the trees, green leaves shaking against each other. As in all places where they grow, the aspens here were pioneering a recently disturbed area, in this case a combination of rockslides and avalanches falling from the steep valley walls above. If there was any doubt we were in a mid-montane, Canadian-type forest, this sight dispelled it. Not only was this forest similar to those of the north in terms of its climatic conditions, structure, and functions of species, but actual species were the same. This was the very same *Populus tremuloides* found in the Canadian-type forests of Alaska, all the way across the North Woods to Maine.

The last stretch was a grunt up the steep riser and through the trees. Soaked with sweat and covered in dirt and debris from bushwhacking, we let our packs drop and roll across the blessed flat slabs of granite that meant camp.

For three days we studied the ecology of pollination while watching rufous hummingbirds draw nectar from Newberry's penstemons. We discussed and debated the ecological causes and potential value of the diversity of life on earth while observing innumerable species of wildflowers, turning our heads upside-down to peek into the corollas of crimson columbines. We studied the evolutionary characteristics of mammals while fending off *Ursus americana*, the ubiquitous black bear of the Sierra Nevada. After all that, it was time to ascend another three thousand feet, through the uppermost montane forest and into the land above the trees. With our packs three days lighter and the wide expanse of the alpine Sierra Nevada on our minds, we rose to the task at hand.

Ascending the glacial staircase from our camp at nine thousand feet, we strained our legs once again and wound our way up the steep granite slabs and through the trees. As the riser we had camped against rounded out to the next tread, we came to the marshy shore of a shallow lake, nestled like a babe in the cradling arms of granite. Here, the undulating glacial ice of the Pleistocene had carved out a small basin, the way a waterfall does when it falls down a steep slope and abruptly meets a flat bed. Since the ice had pulled back, the lake had slowly but surely filled in with sediments washed down from the heights above. The banks of the lake were lined with willows, tolerant of the fluctuating lake levels and prolonged periods of innundation. Further in from the shore, rooted aquatic plants grew, their foliage suspiciously floating on the water's surface. As the sediments washed in, the lake grew increasingly shallow, its waters displaced outward as it simultaneously grew wider. We peered down through the surface at dozens of submerged logs, trees that had once lined the lake and collapsed into its waters as they widened. Mosquitoes whirred around us by the hundreds, urging us to keep going up, above the trees and into the wind. We might have been in Alaska, or deep in the lake country of Ontario, Manitoba, and Quebec. We could have been in Scotland, on the shore of some haunted loch, or chasing reindeer herds across northern Scandinavia. But this was the Sierra Nevada, and one look above the lodgepole pines that lined the lake revealed the walls of bright granite mountains. The glacier that carved this basin was no sprawling gargantuan continental ice sheet, but a steep and undulating mountain glacier. We were not in the boreal forests of the north, but rather the upper montane forest of the Sierra Nevada of California.

Two more risers and another lake later, we emerged from the trees into the wide open sunlit space of the High Sierra. At just below eleven thousand feet, it was unusual for the trees to open up so low, and sure enough, as we traversed the shores of Sphinx Lakes, sporadic trees continued to make appearances all the way up to twelve thousand feet. We crossed granite slabs glistening in the sun, worn and polished by the undersides of glaciers long past, striations etched into their shining surfaces by the rocks and sand that were once pressed between the rock and the overbearing ice. We crunched our way across extensive gravel flats, where drought-resistant pussypaws and wild buckwheats eked out a living. Bright green ribbons of dense vegetation burst forth from the ground just a few feet away, where snowmelt water gurgled in countless threaded streams and delivered moisture all summer long. Flowers grew here in lavish numbers, and insects buzzed through the air. In between were dry and moist meadows, rich with sedges and early flowering dwarf bilberries and kalmias. Snowfields persisted in nooks and crannies, covering the north and east-facing slopes, melting in the heat of summer and watering the ground. Here was the tundra, where small is beautiful and a closer look reveals miniature worlds.

Tucked into a rock crevice at eleven thousand feet, just up from the lower Sphinx Lakes, a cluster of columbines caught our attention. Unlike the bright red nodding flower of the crimson columbine, so common along streamsides in the montane forest, this plant bore larger, paler flowers, creamy whitish-yellow with rosy streaks. Its flowers faced sideways, rather than down, with only half the nod of their montane counterpart. Where they were growing was different as well. This was no streamside, but a rock cranny. Leaving the matter for speculation, we continued ascending.

We kept climbing, from treads filled with sparkling lakes to steep risers of big granite. At 11,500 feet, we began our final climb across old glacial moraine and huge chunks of angular talus, picking our way carefully, slowly but surely, to an obscure pass at over 12,000 feet. Our journey north was complete, and if not for the serrated peaks surrounding us on all sides, we might have been in the arctic, the midnight sun just coming down from its midsummer apex, spiraling around the polar skies. Merriam's theory, just a theory before, became as solid in our experience of the world as eating and breathing. Elevation really did simulate latitude, and the truth was written across every feature of the snow-crusted tundra-graced alpine zone.

Resting there over food and drink, we gazed southeast across yet another basin to a long ridge off the high summit of Mt. Brewer. Along that ridge there was an obvious col, a low saddle carved by glaciers long ago. Through that col was our next camp.

On our way up to the col, a few of us gathered around a familiar sight. It was a columbine, familiar and yet different than the others we had seen before. This one had large, purely pale, cream-colored flowers that grew erect, with no detectable nod. It was growing at the edge of a gravel flat, tucked and shaded against a large granite boulder. We compared it to the columbines below. The crimson had a bright red, nodding, tight, relatively small flower, half the size of this one, and grew along streambanks. This one had a looser, pale cream, erect and relatively large flower, twice the size of its crimson relative, and it grew in rocky places. The columbine at Sphinx Creek was somewhere in the middle. Were we looking at two different species? Speculations arose which quickly turned to hypotheses. We discussed them as we continued ascending. Somehow, engaging in a dialogue about evolution kept us going. Clearly this new columbine, at nearly twelve thousand feet, was no crimson columbine, but something different, perhaps unique to the alpine zone. But what about the Sphinx Lake columbine? Was it an unusual crimson or more akin to the new flower? Was it a third species, unique in its own right? We were looking at evolution in action and we knew it.

For the majority of our time on earth, humans have perceived the world around them as a set creation, made by a creator and set in motion complete. Judeo-Christian mythologies, though often criticized for perpetuating this belief system, are but one of innumerable mythos that reflect the worldview of humans for thousands of years. What on earth would make people believe anything different? Even today, only a handful of scientists have actually seen organic evolution happening, and this has been among organisms so small they are invisible to the naked eye. Yet, we witness such evolution in action everyday, all the time. Every time an organism is born, dies, or engages in reproductive activity, evolution is at work, ever changing the face of life as it moves into tomorrow.

Charles Darwin published his monumental work, *Origin of Species*, in 1859, revolutionizing biology and forever changing the way we view the world. In this work, Darwin articulated the process of natural selection as the mechanism by which species evolve over time. Not only did Darwin provide the mechanism by which species evolve, but he also gave overwhelming evidence to support such evolution of species. In light of the Newtonian-mechanistic worldview that dominated western culture at the time, Darwin's assertion was bold because it suggested that rather than a predictable mechanistic universe, we lived in a dynamic, changing one. This re-infused western thought with a teleological sense of purpose that it had lacked since the Greco-Roman era. Like Merriam, Darwin was a spokesperson for ideas that had been on the table for some time.

During the fifteenth century, Europe was hemmed into a tight corner. To the north were frozen wastes. To the east and south the iron curtain of Islam hacked and hewed at all but a few westerners who penetrated its ever-growing boundary. To the west was the mighty Atlantic, stretching further than the eye could see to the edge of the world. When these confines were finally breached and explorers began pulling into their home harbors laden with otherworldly specimens and descriptions of exotic lands, the very foundations of western thought began to shake and tremble. Where were these species during the great flood of Noah? Were they on board the ark? How could they possibly have all fit? How could God have done all this in just six days? Although they may seem like trite questions to us today, these and many other like questions posed serious challenges to the church-state that shaped the western mind. As science gained credence, further biological and geological discoveries came filing in. Naturalists were perplexed by the similarities between analogous body parts of different organisms. The human hand, the flippers of marine mammals, and the wings of bats shared structural similarities that seemed beyond mere coincidence. The bony protrusions in the rear of the human pelvis corresponded suspiciously to the bony parts of tails. During the early stages of development, human embryos looked just like hundreds of other organisms, including fish. Deep below the surface of the earth, early geologists discovered fossilized marine organisms. The organisms were more simple the deeper they dug, becoming increasingly complex towards the surface. The deeper rocks were older, and this suggested that marine organisms were becoming more and more complex as time progressed. If creation was complete and all species had remained the same since creation was set in motion, how could this be?

By nightfall, over cups of tea and the flush of alpine glow on the west face of South Guard, my students unraveled the mystery of the columbines. The crimson was the elder of the genus *Aquilegia*. As the mountains rose, a new species began to diverge from the crimson columbine in response to the changing environmental conditions, eventually giving rise to a new species. This new species, the Colville's columbine, is more successful in the rocky conditions that dominate the alpine Sierra. Because it grows higher, where the growing season is shorter and pollination activity less, its flowers are larger, erect, and less strictly colored so it can attract a wider variety of pollinators than its crimson cousin. The Sphinx Creek columbine was a hybrid, with characteristics of both species, and evidence that their divergence is both recent and incomplete.

My students were seeing how all life evolved from other life, how new species do not spontaneously appear on earth but arise as modified versions of previous species. I smiled, immeasurably proud of them for tackling such a sophisticated riddle, knowing that this would all lead to more and bigger questions.

Acknowledgements

The genesis of this book was a call to action by Prescott College President, Dan Garvey: "I propose we assemble a book of personal reflections and experiences on being an experiential educator. What have you done? What's worked? What's failed? What's been personally rewarding? Imagine your reader is a faculty member at another institution and she's interested in making a class or position more powerful. What can you share with this audience?" It is because of Dan's vision and support that this book exists.

Were it not for the encouragement and recommendations of Melanie Bishop and K.L. Cook, I would not have found my way onto this project. And were it not for the encouragement and support of my wife, Julie Hensley, who could envision how wonderful this book would turn out before I could, I may not have taken on this project.

There are several other people—friends, former colleagues, and current ones—with whom I dialogued, asked a question, or shared a frustration. For all of these people, named and unnamed, I am thankful. And to all of these people, I am indebted.

About the Editor

R. Dean Johnson is a former fiction editor at *Hayden's Ferry Review*. He has taught composition, creative nonfiction, and fiction at Kansas State University, The University of Alabama, Arizona State University, and Prescott College. His essays and stories have appeared in several journals including *Ascent*, *F. Scott Fitzgerald Review*, *New Orleans Review*, and *Santa Clara Review*.